FOUCAULT, POWER,
AND EDUCATION

STEPHEN J. BALL

INSTITUTE OF EDUCATION, UNIVERSITY OF LONDON

Routledge
Taylor & Francis Group

NEW YORK AND LONDON

First published 2013
by Routledge
711 Third Avenue, New York, NY 10017

Simultaneously published in the UK
by Routledge
2 Park Square, Milton Park, Abingdon, Oxon OX14 4RN

Routledge is an imprint of the Taylor & Francis Group, an informa business

© 2013 Taylor & Francis

The right of Stephen J. Ball to be identified as the author of this work has been
asserted by him in accordance with sections 77 and 78 of the Copyright, Designs
and Patents Act 1988.

All rights reserved. No part of this book may be reprinted or reproduced or utilised
in any form or by any electronic, mechanical, or other means, now known or
hereafter invented, including photocopying and recording, or in any information
storage or retrieval system, without permission in writing from the publishers.

Trademark notice: Product or corporate names may be trademarks or registered
trademarks, and are used only for identification and explanation without intent
to infringe.

Library of Congress Cataloguing in Publication Data
Ball, Stephen J.
Foucault, power, and education / by Stephen J. Ball. – 1st ed.
  p. cm. – (Routledge key ideas in education series)
Includes bibliographical references and index.
1. Foucault, Michel, 1926-1984. 2. Education–Philosophy. 3. Education–Social
aspects. I. Title.
LB880.F682B35 20102
370.1–dc23   2012022266

ISBN: 978-0-415-89536-1 (hbk)
ISBN: 978-0-415-89537-8 (pbk)
ISBN: 978-0-203-07866-2 (ebk)

Typeset in Minion
by Cenveo Publisher Services

Certified Sourcing
www.sfiprogram.org
SFI-00453

Printed and bound in the United States of America
by Edwards Brothers, Inc.

FOUCAULT, POWER,

AND EDUCATION

Foucault, Power, and Education invites internationally-renowned scholar Stephen J. Ball to reflect on the importance and influence of Foucault on his work in educational policy. By focusing on some of the ways Foucault has been placed in relation to educational questions or questions about education, Ball highlights the relationships between Foucault's concepts and methods, and educational research and analysis. An introductory chapter offers a brief explanation of some of Foucault's key concerns, while additional chapters explore ways in which Ball himself has sought to apply Foucault's ideas in addressing contemporary educational issues.

In this intensely personal and reflective text, Ball offers an interpretation of his Foucault—That is, his own particular reading of the Foucauldian toolbox. Ideal for courses in education policy and education studies, this valuable teaching resource is essential reading for any education scholar looking for a starting point into the literature and ideas of Foucault.

Stephen Ball is Karl Mannheim Professor of Sociology of Education, Institute of Education, University of London.

Routledge Key Ideas in Education Series

Series Editors: Greg Dimitriadis and Bob Lingard

Freud and Education, Deborah P. Britzman
Marx and Education, Jean Anyon
Globalization and Education, Fazal Rizvi

Very much for TFG

CONTENTS

SERIES EDITORS' INTRODUCTION

This series introduces key people and topics and discusses their particular implications for the field of education. Written by the most prominent thinkers in the field, these "key ideas" are read through the series' authors' past and present work, with particular attention given to the ways these ideas can, do, and might impact theory, research, practice, and policy in education.

More specifically, these texts offer particular conversations with prominent authors, whose work has resonated across education and related fields. Books in this series read as conversations with authorities, whose thinking has helped constitute these ideas and their role in the field of education—yesterday, today, and tomorrow.

Much more than introductions alone, these short, virtuosic volumes look to shape ongoing discussions in the field of education by putting the field's contemporary luminaries in dialogue with its foundational figures and critical topics. From new students to senior scholars, these volumes will spark the imaginations of a range of readers thinking through key ideas and education.

Greg Dimitriadis, University at Buffalo,
SUNY, USA, and Bob Lingard,
The University of Queensland, Australia

PREFACE

And if I don't ever say what must be done, it isn't because I believe that there's nothing to be done; on the contrary, it is because I think that there are a thousand things to do, to invent, to forge, on the part of those who, recognizing the relations of power in which they're implicated, have decided to resist or escape them. From this point of view all of my investigations rest on a postulate of absolute optimism.

(Foucault, 1991b Remarks on Marx)

This book is full of loose ends, compromises and missed opportunites. There are many gestures towards possibilities that are not taken up but to which I hope to return, it is an adventure and a transgression, a beginning. If I can borrow Foucault's famous sentence, he said 'I don't write a book so that it will be the final word; I write a book so that other books are possible, not necessarily written by me'. Paul Veyne likens coming to grips with Foucault as like climbing a mountain, but during which there are moments when 'one is happy to feel one's crampons biting into the ice on slopes covered in shifting snow' (2010 p.66). I did have some such happy moments, and I hope you the reader may experience a few.

As I wrote I was reminded by colleagues of the need to 'name-check' and refer, and the dangers of treading on the territories of others without due acknowledgement. I am very aware that I have not always done those things – sorry about that. Certainly I have not paid enough attention to the ways in which Critical Race Theory, feminisms and disability studies have been in the forefront of the sort of 'unsettling' work I outline and have as a result changed the shape of policies and truths in education.

Many people have contributed to the writing of this book directly and indirectly. I am particularly grateful to the series editors Greg Dimitriardis and Bob Lingard for their constructive comments, and to my research student reading group for their patience. I also had very positive feedback and support from: Julie Allan, Felicity Armstrong, Patrick Bailey, Trinidad Ball, Pablo del Monte, Dave Gillborn, Emiliano Grimaldi, Jane McKay, Meg Maguire, Jane Martin, Paula Mena, Antonio Olmedo, Jane Perryman, Nicola Rollock, Diego Santori, Roger Slee, Carol Vincent and Deborah Youdell. They were all very kind to go to much trouble. I have not always done full justice to their concerns.

FIGURES AND BOX

1

DO WE REALLY NEED ANOTHER BOOK ABOUT FOUCAULT?

Jana Sawicki describes speaking with Foucault at a seminar in Vermont in 1983:

> I told him that I had just finished writing a dissertation on his critique of humanism. Not surprisingly, he responded with some embarrassment and much seriousness. He suggested that I not spend energy talking about him and, instead, do what he was doing, namely, write genealogies.
>
> (Sawicki, 1991, p. 15)

I do not "do Foucault", and I am not a Foucauldian. Not that such a thing makes sense, as I shall try to explain and demonstrate. Indeed I no longer have much interest in being a *something*—that is in claiming allegiance to some orthodoxy or community of like-minded scholars committed to a single theoretical position. Rather, I am more interested in the crafting of an academic subject yet to come. For a significant period of my academic career I was searching for a sense of identity and security. I wanted to work nicely and productively within a set of historical conditions of thought that I would never need to consider very seriously or challenge. I wanted to find some body of thought or some key thinker or ideas within which I could feel comfortable and to which or to whom I could turn for the solution to my analytic difficulties and struggles for sense and meaning. Being a *something*, being a "wise fool", seemed to have many attractions and advantages. I might have been, at various times, a Weberian, or symbolic interactionist, or critical ethnographer, enfolded gently in their affirmations and "transcendental teleologies" (Foucault, 1972), but only might. I was never quite certain enough, so the fact of my identity was never quite established. Reading Foucault put a stop to all of that. Reading Foucault was a struggle and a shock but also a revelation, indeed Charles Taylor begins an essay on Foucault with the words "Foucault disconcerts" (1986, p. 69). Many of his substantive ideas have become of great importance to me in the empirical work I have done on educational processes, institutions and policies, as I will describe and explore later. However, equally important to me is Foucault's stance and style of work, the kind of scholar and intellectual he was, and his own struggles not to be "a something". That is, the particular ethics of intellectual work as a practice of self that he undertook. Indeed his work is defined by his attempts to find a position outside of the human sciences from which to see the social world, and to see the human sciences as a part of that social world—a space that is both liberating and impossible (see Chapter 4). Veyne (2010) had intended to call his book about Foucault "the goldfish bowl and the samurai". Foucault's intellectual project rested on seeking to find a space beyond traditional disciplinary or theoretical positions, from which he could subject those positions to analysis and critique, and trouble the "inscription of progress" in modern politics and scholarship. He set himself staunchly against the notion of a universal or self-evident humanity. As Popkewitz and Brennan (1998) put it "For our purposes, Foucault offers the possibility of a different kind of theoretical and political project, which does not automatically privilege its own position." This is definitely not comfortable and affirming, it involves, as Burchell explains "the experience of not being a citizen of the community or republic of thought and action in which one nevertheless is unavoidably implicated or involved" (1996, p. 30). There is a dual ambivalence here, one aspect in relation to scholarship and one in relation to the practices of government and the constant challenge of "not knowing what and how to think" (Burchell, 1996, p. 30). It involves finding ways to work in the tensions between technologies of competence and technologies of the self. Reading Foucault has made me question what I do as a scholar and social critic, and ethically who I am and what I might become. I have had to confront not the ways in which I am determined but rather the ways in which I might be revocable. He makes me uneasy, in a productive and generative way. He has unsettled my sense of the claims I might make about my work, its purposes, and its role in the enterprise of modernist human science, although I revert to that enterprise regularly and with ease, often with a sigh of relief. In many respects Foucault only really makes sense when his substantive works are viewed, read, understood in relation to his refusal to accept the inscriptions and limits and structures of "normal" social science. As Oksala suggests: "To get closer to Foucault's intent, it helps if one is willing to question the ingrained social order, give up all truths firmly fixed in stone, whilst holding on to a fragile commitment to freedom" (2007, p. 1). Foucault, although he is often read in a rather different way, is all about being free but also about the dangers of freedom. "My role" he said "is to show people that they are much freer than they feel ..." (Martin et al., 1988, p. 10). His work questions the meaning of freedom, and he sets himself against the idea of freedom as a state of being. Foucault tends to be read by many as an historian of power, discipline, subjectification and normalization, whose work produces a sense of the impossibility of freedom, but that is dangerously misleading and one-sided. He was as much concerned with the modalities of freedom as he was with the production of docility. Perhaps with some exaggeration, Mendieta argues that "Genealogy it could be said, is a science of freedom ..." (2011, p. 113). This raises issues about both subjectivity and scholarship to which I will return briefly at the end of the book. Most of all, for me, Foucault's work continues to provide a set of effective tools for intervening within contemporary discourses of power. As he explained: "Everything I do, I do in order that it may be of use" (Defert & Ewald, 2001, pp. 911–912). His histories in particular are intended "to show that things weren't as necessary as all that" (Foucault, 1991a, p. 76) and thus why "they are not as necessary as all that", now. All of this can be confusing and difficult if we attempt to read Foucault as just another enlightenment scholar or just another post-structuralist. To do so is impoverishing of him and of the reader. The challenge is not to agree with Foucault but to be disconcerted by him, to be made to think in new spaces and to consider new possibilities for thought. However, as I said, I am not a Foucauldian; indeed, much of my research and writing remains focused on the "problem of meaning" and draws upon actors' accounts of the social world as the basis for interpreting and explaining the social—I dabble in the mysterious and modernist arts of ethnography. Foucault's work, in stark contrast, begins with "the unconscious structures of thought" and the organizing discourses which operate at an archaeological (rules and regularities) rather than an epistemological (claims to truth) level of knowledge. While the latter seeks to separate the objects and subjects of knowledge and establish a relation to "truth", the former addresses how a particular discourse acquires the status of scientificity, how it creates in itself, so to speak, the conditions of what counts as truth.

> I tried to explore scientific discourse not from the point of view of the individuals who are speaking, nor from the point of view of the formal structures of what they are saying, but from the point of view of the rules that come into play in the very existence of such discourse: what conditions did Linnaeus (or Petty, or Arnauld) have to fulfill, not to make his discourse coherent and true in general, but to give it, at the time when it was written and accepted, value and practical application as scientific discourse.
>
> (Foucault, 1970b, p. xiv)

He was profoundly and consistently interested in how "human beings are made subjects" (Foucault, 1982, p. 208) but not interested in "speaking subjects" per se. Indeed he saw the modern preoccupation with self, what he called "anthropological prejudice", as an inhibition to the possibilities of thought: "It is no longer possible to think in our days other than in the void left by man's disappearance" (Foucault, 1970b, p. 34). This void is, he goes on to say, "nothing more, nothing less, than the unfolding space in which it is once more possible to think". I explored with Maria Tamboukou, some of the continuities, affinities and contradictions embedded in the tensions between discourse and hermeneutics in a book we edited, *Dangerous Encounters: Genealogy and Ethnography* (Tamboukou & Ball, 2004). Among many other things both genealogists and ethnographers are fascinated by the minutiae of everyday life and the ways in which the sinews of power are embedded in mundane practices and in social relationships and the haphazard and contingent nature of practices. This was never more clear to me than in the work I have done on "performativity", in looking at the ways in which lists, forms, grids and rankings work to change the meaning of educational practice—what it means to teach and learn—and our sense of who we are in terms of these practices—what it means to be an educator, and to be educated, I return to these concerns in Chapter 4. The focus of much of Foucault's work is on such practices and on power relations[1] and on the problem of government. In his "middle period" in particular his attention was focused on the "management of populations" and on what he called "bio-power"—of which education is a significant component—and this is addressed in Chapter 2. He was interested in the ways in which power flows through architecture, organizational arrangements, professional expertise and knowledge, systems of classification and "dividing practices", therapeutic procedures and how it comes to be written onto bodies and into our conduct—that is, power as totalizing and individualizing and as productive. As he wrote "Power produces, it produces reality" (Foucault, 1979, p. 194).

When I am stuck with a problem of analysis, I will often turn to Foucault, and read something, anything, relevant or not. He unclutters my mind, enables me to think differently, in new spaces and to escape from the analytic clichés, which are so prevalent in contemporary sociological work. I also often find his writing elegant and engaging, and although I have never sought to write like him, he has again changed the way I write and the way I think about writing, about "the author function" and the process of the production of texts. Indeed, Foucault was preoccupied with writing, and described it as "like a game that invariably goes beyond its own rules and transgresses it limits" (Foucault, 1998, p. 206). He attributed great importance to the act of writing as a practice of freedom and in a very late paper explored the possibilities of what he called "self writing" (Foucault, n.d.), that is a process of self-shaping through the production of texts. "When I write I do it above all to change myself and not to think the same thing as before" (Foucault, 1991b, p. 27). In this way he was clear about how he approached intellectual problems and approached writing. He regarded his intellectual endeavours as a way of working on himself; he was always a work in progress, always unfinished, restless and angry. Our task each day, he suggested, is to decide that which is of the greatest danger, and explained:

> My point is not that everything is bad, but that everything is dangerous, which is not exactly the same as bad. If everything is dangerous, then we always have something to do. So my position leads not to apathy but to a hyper- and pessimistic activism.
>
> (Foucault, 1983c, pp. 231–232, see Chapter 4)

While we read Foucault as a writer, it is important to recognize that Foucault was a speaking scholar as much as a writing scholar, indeed there were long gaps between his books (for example, from the publication in France of *The Archaeology of Knowledge* in 1969 to *Discipline and Punish* in 1975, from the *History of Sexuality Volume 1* in 1976 to *Volumes 2 and 3* 1984) and he announced many plans for books which were never realized. He was a writer, researcher, journalist, political activist and serial interviewee. However, for 12 of the 13 years he was a professor at the College de France he gave an annual series of 12 lectures on Wednesdays, from January to March, which are now translated into English and published. These lectures involved the presentation of new work and work in progress, they attracted large audiences, typically around 500 people, and he spoke from behind a forest of cassette recorders —a setting that he did not enjoy. In 1976 he changed the time of the lectures to try to reduce the attendance—to no avail:

> Foucault approached his teaching as a researcher: explorations for a future book as well as the opening up of fields of problematisation were formulated as an invitation to possible future researchers. This is why the courses at the College de France do not duplicate the published books. ... They have their own status.
>
> (Ewald and Fontona, Introduction to Foucault, 2010a, p. xiv)

In these lectures he "anticipates, intersects with, and develops themes and analyses found in his published books" (Davidson, 2003, p. xvii). The lectures used history and philosophy from a phenomenal range of sources to provide perspective on contemporary events. They also represent a set of explorations in the genealogy of power/knowledge relations, which was his main philosophical and analytic preoccupation from 1970 on, as distinct from, to some extent, his previous work on the archeology of discursive formations. Apart from the lectures, Foucault also gave many interviews both to journalists and to academics and held Q&A sessions with students, which he seemed to enjoy, and towards the end of his life he gave a series of lectures at Berkeley and Vermont on "truth telling" and "the care of the self". In the lectures, especially those at the College de France, Foucault makes some of his reasoning and his "methods" clearer than in the written texts. He used the lectures to build and try out arguments and lines of inquiry. For example, referring back to his studies of the genealogy of madness he explains:

> My question was not: Does madness exist? My reasoning, my method, was not to examine whether history gives me or refers me to something like madness, and then to conclude, no, it does not, therefore madness does not exist. This was not the argument, the method in fact. The method consisted in saying: Let's suppose that madness does not exist. If we suppose that it does not exist, then what can history make of these different events and practices which are apparently organised around something that is supposed to be madness? So what I would like to deploy here is exactly the opposite of historicism: not, then, questioning universals by using history as a critical method, but starting from the decision that universals do not exist, asking what kind of history we can do.
>
> (Foucault, 2010a, p. 3, lecture, 10 January 1979)

As indicated already, Foucault spent a great deal of time and energy avoiding being or being seen or positioned as a structuralist, post-structuralist (he claimed not to know what that meant), historian, philosopher, or postmodernist, or even bizarrely a Marxist, or anti-Marxist. In many interviews he was asked "what he was" and thus "who he was", questions he usually refused or evaded.

> I'm very proud that some people think that I'm a danger for the intellectual health of students. When people start thinking of health in intellectual activities, I think there is something wrong. In their opinion I am a dangerous man, since I am a crypto-Marxist, an irrationalist, a nihilist.
>
> (Interview, 25 October 1982 [Foucault, 1988d])

In an often-used quotation, he said, and this relates back to my starting point above:

> I don't feel that it is necessary to know exactly what I am. The main interest in life and work is to become someone else that you were not in the beginning. If you knew when you began a book what you would say at the end, do you think that you would have the courage to write it? What is true for writing and for a love relationship is true also for life. The game is worthwhile insofar as we don't know what will be the end. My field is the history of thought. Man is a thinking being.
>
> (Martin et al., 1998, p. 9)

As often noted he insisted on inventing his own professorial title at the College de France—Professor of the History of Systems of Thought—he did not want to signal any allegiance to traditional lines of thought. He also drew on many diverse philosophical and theoretical influences; Plato, St Augustine, Nietzsche, Heidegger, Canguilhem, Dumezil, Hyppolite, Weber, Kant and others—his erudition is frightening.

In relation to this diverse but substantial *oeuvre* the issue of what he called "the author function" is fascinating to contemplate. The author he argued is a category and a way of organizing texts, which has its own history; the "author function" is a set of beliefs or assumptions governing the production, circulation, classification and consumption of texts. In effect, the term "author" does not refer simply to a real individual. In this vein, in the Introduction to *The Archaeology of Knowledge* he says "I am no doubt not the only one who writes in order to have no face" (Foucault, 1974, p. 17), although his face, the Foucault brand, is well known (I have a Foucault mug) and indeed his authorship is rarely in doubt. Indeed, Foucault is a very present author "in" his texts, he often speaks to us directly but also sometimes subverts the "normal" organization of scholarly texts, and he developed his own tropes and techniques of argument. He also made extensive use of metonym and metaphor and often alludes to internecine debates within French intellectual life without much contextual explanation. As one critic admits, Foucault's own discourse is a "labyrinth into which I can venture … in which I can lose myself" (Midelfort, 1980, p. 249), what hope for the rest of us. Mahon (1992, p. 62) writes of "the quagmire of Foucault's turgid prose" but also notes that at times his style becomes "positively poetic"—the final sentence of the *The Order of Things* is a good example. He was often disconcertingly honest about his work and his own evaluation of it, particularly in his lecture series at the College de France. He writes in the Introduction to *The Archaeology of Knowledge*:

> Hence the cautious, stumbling manner of this text: at every turn, it stands back, measures up what is before it, gropes towards its limits, stumbles against what it does not mean, and digs pits to mark out its own path.

(1974, p. 17)[2]

At the beginning of the second part of *The Archeology of Knowledge* (135), reviewing his progress thus far, he says: "I have appealed to a whole apparatus, whose sheer weight and, no doubt, bizarre machinery are a source of embarrassment." Most people who set out to read the book would find it hard to disagree with him. The final chapter of *The Archaeology of Knowledge* takes the form of a dialogue with himself, or perhaps with the reader, in which he responds to a series of challenges and difficult questions. Indeed, he often exercised the "author function" in a very individual and assertive way, for example in his preface to the English edition of *The Order of Things*.

All of this sometimes makes his work "difficult" to read, it has to be read on its own terms. Nonetheless his texts are also "writerly" texts, that is they include an invitation to participate in the thinking about a problem, to engage in the co-production of ideas. He leaves open points of entry for the reader to bring meaning to bear but never makes things easy. He is always trying out ideas, going off on tangents. He is sometimes elliptical and obscure, particularly when he is seeking within his writing to find ways of expressing himself which do not collapse back into the techniques and pre-suppositions from which he is trying to escape and which he is trying to bring into critical view. In all of this, words are important to Foucault, he plays with them and uses them with great care, with different meanings and sometimes he changes what they mean. The words he uses need to be considered with care— and there are sometimes problems with translation. He often uses words in a double sense, to signal paradoxes or to explore relationships between things—for example and most obviously the word *knowledge*, which is sometimes intended to convey the sense of *savoir* (to know a field of knowledge) and at other times *connaissance* (modalities of knowledge). Both meanings come together when knowledge is deployed as *knowledge about* and *knowledge of,* that is the use of science, expertise and technique *to know* subjects. Expertise, like psychiatry, penology, psychology are deployed to construct truths about the subject who is brought into their gaze, who is thus *known* through the methods of observation, testing, appraisal, etc. A great deal of Foucault's works focus on the connection between power relations and the formation of social scientific knowledges, and this fundamental intertwinement is what Foucault refers to by the hybrid *power/knowledge.* "Foucault characterizes power/knowledge as an abstract force which determines what will be known, rather than assuming that individual thinkers develop ideas and knowledge" (Mills, 2003, p. 70). These knowledges, the human sciences he calls them, within which "the subject itself is posited as an object of possible knowledge" (Gutting, 1994, p. 315), developed, he argues, in tandem with specific practices of power—such as the clinic, the prison, the school. The production of knowledge is also a claim for power. These practices or techniques of power are validated within more or less coherent systems of knowledge, which also shape the way we think about illness or criminality or learning. Again there is a duality—an internal focus on the ways in which scientific knowledges are produced, the social construction of scientific truths or material conditions of thought, and an external focus on the ways in which these knowledges produce classes and categories of subjects, endowed with specific characteristics and requiring particular forms of intervention or practices. He sought to work therefore at the nexus where the history of practices meets the history of knowledges. The intertwining of the two within praxis is the distinctive move of genealogy. These knowledges bring into being something that did not exist previously—the hysteric, the delinquent, the idiot child—but, as noted already, refer to something that really exists in the world "which was the target of social regulation at a given moment" (Foucault, 1983a, lecture 6, p. 2). Thus, for example, Foucault contends that sexuality as a term "did not appear until the beginning of the nineteenth century" (Foucault, 1981) and he casts doubt upon what he calls "the repressive hypothesis" as a way of understanding sexuality. Rather, he argued, we need to look at the proliferation of discourses concerned with sex—"a discursive ferment that gathered momentum from the eighteenth century onward" (Foucault, 1981, p. 18). Far from silence, we witness:

> ... an institutional incitement to speak about [sex], and to do so more and more; a determination on the part of the agencies of power to hear it spoken about, and to cause it to speak through explicit articulation and endlessly accumulated detail.
>
> (1981, p. 18)

The effect of all this rational discourse about sex was the increasing encroachment of state law into the realm of private desire:

> one had to speak of [sex] as of a thing to be not simply condemned or tolerated but managed, inserted into systems of utility, regulated for the greater good of all, made to function according to an optimum. Sex was not something one simply judged; it was a thing one administered.
>
> (1981, p. 24)

Such discourses and the expert knowledges in which they are spoken constitute the object of their "concern"—here we could say they were concerned *with* and concerned *about*. Indeed, the human sciences are often about the professionalizing of care and caring—Foucault devoted a number of lectures to the issue of care. The practitioner, the professional, is also brought into being by the knowledge that makes them expert. A key constituent in the formation of the modern state is the production of state professionals who operated on the power/knowledge cusp. Knowledges are produced within power relations also in the sense that some groups or institutions have been able to speak *knowledgeably about* "others", subaltern groups, who were concomitantly rendered silent—men speak about women, deracialized whites about racialized others, heterosexuals about homosexuals, the West about the Orient.

However, Foucault's point is not that we should take for granted the relations entwining power and knowledge but rather that those relations need to be explored in every case. Furthermore, to grasp the reach and force of Foucault's project the *subject* needs to be inserted between power/knowledge. That is to say, power relations are always instantiated in certain "fields of knowledge, types of normativity and forms of subjectivity" (1992, p. 4). Experts and their knowledges play a key role in determining how we should act and who we are. But I digress, and these power/subject/knowledge relationships are very much the focus of Chapters 2 and 3. What I am highlighting here are some of the difficulties involved in taking Foucault seriously. He upsets, in both senses, many of the key working principles of modern social scientific thought. In particular, he challenges our preoccupation with and allegiance to the constituting subject. In *The Archaeology of*

Knowledge, Foucault wrote about wanting to "cleanse" history of "transcendental narcissism" (1974, p. 203). In other words, the subject itself has a history, "the subject emerges within discourse the individual is not a pre-given entity" (Foucault, 1980, p. 73). The interplay between knowledge, power and subjectivity is very nicely explained by Foucault in an interview with Paul Rabinow in 1984, where he describes his work on madness, delinquency and sexuality as involving "the establishment of a certain objectivity, the development of a politics and a government of the self, and the elaboration of an ethics and a practice in regard to oneself" (p. 4). Knowledge is always an ethical as well as a political practice.

Prado (1995) suggests that the best way to read Foucault (and I would agree) is to begin in the middle. It is very tempting, and many have succumbed, to order Foucault into three periods, three sets of preoccupations and three "methods"—archeology, genealogy and technologies of the self—although Dreyfus and Rabinow offer four! There is some sense to this; it is not "outside the true". The work can usefully be "broken" down into these phases, and indeed, to a great extent I am going to organize the remainder of this book around these phases, or a version of them. Foucault's work has a developmental trajectory in the sense of building, moving, changing over time, with distinctive points of transition, although some lines of thought were abandoned and dead ends reached. Nonetheless, it would be a mistake to see the transitions as ruptures, as Nealon puts it "rather than seeing his post-1969 shifts of emphasis as a series of failures and dialectical sublations. I'll argue that the shifts in Foucaultian emphasis are more productively understood as a series of 'intensifications'" (2008, p. 5). The secondary literature tends to see Foucault's late period work as an attempt to redress or unpick the supposedly totalizing theoretical cage constructed by his work of discipline and government by attending instead to resistance and self-authorship. As McNay sees it, in the later work:

> Through the formation of a "critical ontology of the self" it is possible to formulate an alternative ethical standpoint from which individuals can begin to resist the normalising force of the "government of individualisation".
>
> (1994, p. 133)

Foucault certainly does not acknowledge this movement in the focus of his work as a break, and his own claims about the integrating principles of his work rest on the topics and questions that preoccupied him rather than the ideas he brought to bear, although (Prado, 1995) cautions that "Foucault's efforts to present his work as more homogenous, coherent and focused than it was should be judiciously assessed." Foucault once asserted, "My work takes place between abutments and anticipatory strings and dots" (1984b, p. 223). There certainly is a sense in which everything he wrote is a set of preludes to something else that remains to be written, and that is always out of grasp.

In 1983 Foucault described his work of the previous 20 years as having been "to create a history of the different modes by which, in our culture, human beings are made subjects" (Dreyfus & Rabinow 1983, p. 208). In the Berkeley lectures also in 1983 (Foucault, 1983a) he said:

> What I tried to do from the beginning was to analyze the process of "problematisation"—which means: how and why certain things, behaviour, phenomena, processes become a problem.
>
> (lecture 6)

He also spoke of his work as being concerned with the history of practices and the history of veridictions or a history of institutions. Foucault certainly did not outline a general theory of society, rather he identified a set of "problems" and outlined some methods of analysis (archaeology and genealogy in particular) and developed a set of tools, a toolbox of concepts, which he hoped others would use and develop further. He expressed frustration that so much effort was devoted to writing about what he might mean rather than doing the sort of practical analytical work that he advocated so vigorously. I am attempting to do some of both here.

Given my rendition of Foucault so far, it is perhaps not surprising, but somewhat paradoxical to say, that Foucault is routinely misread and misused by educational researchers. Prado (1995, p. 3) says that the "cardinal marginality" of Foucault's work and the shifts in his thinking "conspire to invite misinterpretation". Indeed, Foucault's work is subjected to an almost systematic banalization. There is a constant importing of questions, which he wanted to dispense with. Some of his key terms and concepts have been taken up in educational studies and in many other fields and misused and misrepresented to such an extent that they are in some circumstances rendered almost useless. His concepts are routinely deployed in ways that often bear no relation to his intention or meaning.

> Today, analyses employing a Foucauldian perspective can be found throughout the educational research establishment. Foucauldian buzzwords such as "power/knowledge", "panoptic gaze", and "archeology (and/or) genealogy" proliferate in conferences, debates, and journal articles.
>
> (Butin, 2001, pp. 159–160)

Peters and Besley (2007, p. 3) assert that "in the field of education scholars and theorists deform him … they abuse him in countless ways; they unmake and remake him; they twist and turn him and his words …" and Marshall (1989, p. 98) suggests: "it is far from clear that the theoretical radicalness of the work has been grasped". In much of the work that purports to be Foucauldian in educational studies, power is reduced to domination and knowledge is detached from power. Perhaps most common are those studies, which claim to be undertaking some form of Foucauldian discourse analysis, where the object of study is text and language rather than discourse. Many writers claim to being "doing" Foucault and assume that discourses can be accessed and unpacked with a bit of critical detachment and some analysis of key or recurrent words and phrases—although does it matter if it produces useful work?

While, as usual, Foucault uses the term discourse in different ways in his work, most pertinently he was concerned to address the structures and rules that constitute a discourse rather than the texts and utterances produced within it. Discourse is not present in the object, but "enables it to appear". Discourse is the conditions under which certain statements are considered to be the truth. As Mills (2003, p. 55) puts it clearly: "In considering the term 'discourse' we must remember that it is not the equivalent of 'language.'" Discourse is that which constrains *or enables*, writing, speaking and thinking. Foucault once referred to discourse as "the domain of subconscious knowledge" and in *The Archeology of Knowledge*, rather poetically writes that:

> … discourse is secretly based on an "already said"; and that this
> "already said" is not merely a phrase that has been already spoken,

or a text that has been written, but a "never said", an incorporeal discourse, a voice as silent as a breath, a writing that is merely the hollow of its own mark.

(1974, p. 25)

Statements make persons—we do not speak discourse, discourses speak us. Discourses produce the objects about which they speak. He goes on to say:

Of course, discourses are composed of signs; but what they do is more than use these signs to designate things. It is this more that renders them irreducible to the language (langue) and to speech. It is this "more" that we must reveal and describe.

(ibid, p. 49)

We can think about this *more* in a number of different ways; on the one hand Foucault outlined the procedures, which constrain discourse and its production—forms of exclusion— on the other he spoke of the "ponderous, formidable materiality" (Foucault, 1981, p. 52) of discourse. The former takes account of the wider context in which words are uttered— who speaks, from where and in what way, that is, what renders statements possible. But statements are not necessarily speech acts; they can be grids, diagrams and equations. Again this avoids any references to the speaking subjects themselves or to their intention. Foucault also asserts the autonomy of discourse, that language has a power that cannot be reduced to other things, to economic and social forces. In this way, the operation of discursive practices is to make it virtually impossible to think outside of them; to be outside of them is, by definition, to be mad, to be beyond comprehension and therefore reason. The discursive rules that produce and define reason are linked to the exercise of power. The materiality of discourse also draws attention to architectures, organizations, practices and subjects and subjectivities (including the author) as manifestations of discourse, and again underlines the misunderstandings involved in reducing discourse to language.

We also have to think about the relation of discourse to *episteme*. An *episteme*, is a unitary practico-cognitive structure, a regime of truth or general politics of truth, which provides the unconscious codes and rules or holistic conceptual frameworks "that define problematics and their potential resolutions and constitute views of the world comprising the most fundamental of identificatory and explanatory notions, such as the nature of causality in a given range of phenomena" (Prado, 1995, p. 26). That is, an *episteme* establishes the conditions for any statement to be "within the true"—"one would only be in the true, however, if one obeyed the rules of some discursive 'police' which would have to be reactivated every time one spoke" (Foucault, 1970b, p. 31). In a sense discourses (specific ones like psychiatry or general ones like sexuality) are nested within an *episteme*, which makes them possible, and discursive formations and their relationships constitute the *episteme*. There are no transitions or unilinear developments from one *episteme* to another; they are distinguished by discontinuities, changes in the mode of being. The *episteme* is a complex set of relationships between knowledges, an open *dispersion*, a set of rules that "define the objects proper to their own study" (1970b, p. xi) and thus organize how we think, know and write. In *The Order of Things* Foucault examines in painstaking detail the epistemic history in three epochs of what he sees as the three foundational disciplines of the human sciences, linguistics (man speaks), biology (man lives) and economics (man labours). The epochs he identifies are the *renaissance*, the *classical*, beginning in roughly the mid-seventeenth century and the *modern*, beginning in late-eighteenth or early-nineteenth century. As far as we are concerned here it is useful to note at least the conditions of thought, methods and practices and rules for new knowledge that Foucault identifies as underpinning the modern, and specifically bringing into being the possibilities of man, indeed the necessity of man, with whom we will be primarily concerned. Humanity he declared was barely a century old. The attention in *The Order of Things* to scientific practices again highlights the materiality of discourse; that is not just as a form of representation, but as methods and social institutions. Modern man is constituted from what he calls an "empirico-transcendental doublet". Man as a reflexive and transcendental knower is autonomous and rational, but also the product of unconscious forces and cultural practices—which are the stuff of the human sciences. Man is both a source of meaning and a social product, we know ourselves only within the possibilities provided to us by the human sciences as "enslaved sovereign, observed spectator" (1970, p. 323). The limits of knowledge are also the possibilities of knowing. Again this creates great discomforts for many modern scholars who find it difficult to conceive that man is a finite, historical and empirical being that is dated and enfolded in the "discourses" of each epoch, rather a transcendental one.

Most "users" of Foucault avoid or ignore *epistemes*. Many commentaries exclude them; in a way they are too big, too deep and too hard. *The Order of Things*, a best seller when published in France, must be one of the greatest and grandest, but most daunting studies in modern social science. It is a tour de force, breathtaking and mind-numbing in its sweep and ambition but it is as a result stultifying, where do we go with it, what do we do with it?

One writer in educational studies who has tried to take Foucault's archeological method seriously, by outlining a *policy archeology*, that is by viewing *policy as discourse* (Ball, 1993), is Scheurich (1994). In this he seeks to disturb "the tranquility" with which "social problems" are accepted as "natural occurrences" and suggests that policy archeology would address "the historical a priori" (Mahon, 1992, p. 60), that is "the constitutive grid of conditions, assumptions, forces which make the emergence of a social problem" (Scheurich, 1994, p. 300). This "grid of social regularities" constitutes "what becomes socially visible as a social problem and what becomes socially visible as a range of credible policy solutions" (p. 301)—the possible and the impossible (what actors do not think about)—and thus the objects, subjects and concepts that policies form and regulate. Gale (2001, p. 389) tries out Scheurich's approach and goes on to add: "… what is important to uncover is not so much who speaks but what is spoken, what positions it is spoken from [what Foucault called *authorities of delimitation*], and how this is mediated by the speaking positions of others; an architecture of policy positions". This architecture is a frame or field within which divergent discourses, new and old, confront one another, in which some are marginalized or subjugated and others are appropriated to define the "domains of validity, normativity and actuality" (Foucault, 1974, p. 68). Again discourse is related directly to power, to regimes of truth and *grids of specification*—the dividing, contrasting, classifying and relating together of objects of discourse. I will return to this kind of approach in Chapters 2 and 3.

Some periodization is again useful here: from 1970 on, as part of the shift in Foucault's focus of attention from archeology to genealogy, his interest in discourse moves onto a more distinctly political terrain, and this involves asking questions about the institutional production of discourse, as discussed earlier. There is a recombining of the analysis of the epistemic with analysis of the political focused on the concept of power/knowledge. Much of this gets lost in most current work claiming to be discourse analysis. Peters and Besley (2007, p. 1) ask the question: "Why read Foucault today?" and go on to ask: "Is the Foucault we read today institutionally castrated, old and toothless? And have we made him so?" We are certainly in danger in educational studies of stripping out what is challenging and radical from Foucault's work and what makes him worth reading. Peters and Besley go on to argue that, aside from simple misunderstanding, the issue here is one of reception, and that "the question of reception of Foucault needs to be written for specific countries, locations and disciplines ..." (p. 2), and indeed different times. That is to say, different Foucaults have been made up in different cultural and intellectual traditions in different locations, and indeed as indicated above Foucault made himself up differently overtime and we read him differently now from before. Eribon (1991, p. xi), one of his biographers, says "there are several Foucaults—a thousand Foucaults". Peters and Besley provide a useful and accessible introduction to these different Foucaults, and flatteringly and worryingly they see me as having made up the Foucault that "dominates" in "British educational circles", an "ethno-sociological" Foucault.

That brings me back to the issue I have been avoiding thus far in this chapter and that is announced in its title. Do I really want to contribute to the Foucault industry? Do we need another book about Foucault? There are dozens of primers, digests, guides-for-dummies, introductions, overviews, edited collections (I have edited two myself)—I have a considerable collection of these (I count 43) and some are very good—much better than anything I am able to offer. I do not think I have anything new to say about Foucault, how could I? I do not have a new and novel reading of his later work. I have certainly not discovered an unpublished manuscript. I never met Foucault or heard him speak and my French is appalling, I am unable to read him properly in the original. I do have a *Dictionnaire Foucault* (Revel 2008), which I can cope with. Added to which I am a sociologist who has read little philosophy and who, as noted earlier, "grew up" in the hermeneutic tradition. So maybe I should not write this book—but *I want* to write it and the editors and publisher believe that enough people might want to read it. As I have tried to explain Foucault has influenced me and my work, and the way I work in profound ways, although as I have said that does not make me a *Foucauldian*. What I offer is something like a Foucauldian workbook, that is, a set of exercises in analysis that can be used as starting points to address some practical issues in the world of education, some experiments and explorations in the possibilities of at least one Foucault. The book is not "about" Foucault but rather about "doing" Foucault, using his work hopefully in something like the spirit he intended (Foucault, 1988c). These exercises will draw upon some work that I have done and some that I have never been able to do—for example I have been thinking about Foucault and urban education since I moved to King's College in 1985 and this is the main focus of Chapter 2. That said, I want to underline the notion of "starting points", given the space available several of the lines of enquiry which are opened up below are very superficially sketched and will have to be taken further, if they seem interesting, by others. Also I by no means claim all of these openings as original, I will try to use or refer to some of the excellent uses to which Foucault's work has been put already by others. In this enterprise, most of all perhaps, as Alan Sheridan writes in his introduction to *Foucault: The Will to Truth* (1980) my intention is that the book "should create readers" and provoke a need in others to read Foucault's "gleaming words" and to take him seriously.

The book then is about some relations between Foucault's concepts and methods and educational research and analysis and specifically my particular interest in education policy. I will not rehearse in any detail what Foucault had to say about education, which was not much, but I will look at that in passing (see Hunter, 1994; Green, 1998; Deacon, 2006; Marshall, 1989), rather I will address some applications of Foucault's "methods" in relation to educational questions or questions about education. The three chapters which follow will each explore a particular set of questions related to contemporary educational issues, roughly mapped onto Foucault's three major "problematizations". This involves trying things out for size—and there are some loose ends and dead ends—but, to repeat, as Foucault explained in an interview in 1982 "If you knew when you began a book what you would say at the end, do you think you would have the courage to write it?" (Martin et al., 1988, p. 9).

Even if, as I write, I do not know what I will say at the end, I have thought long and hard about how to write the book, how to organize it, what to include and leave out. What I end up with is organized around an interplay between problems and "periods" and a sort of timeline—very traditional history—but this is not so much a structure as a container, a heuristic within which I will attempt to use Foucault and thus, at least to some extent, explain Foucault. A history of problems and practices and an analytics of power and latterly a history of the subject, a "history of the present" as Foucault put it. These practices, institutions and structures constitute objects of study, related to the basic question "what are we now?" and specifically here "what is education policy?". This heuristic is also a way of engaging with what Foucault called his "triple theoretical displacement" (Flynn, 2005, p. 262) of the traditional social sciences. That is Foucault's displacements (Figure 1.1).

These are the terrain of his thinking and his analytic work and if we detach them or isolate them one from the other, we distort and inhibit the possibilities of analysis. That is, "neither are reduced one to the other nor absorbed one by the

Knowledge	> power/knowledge	> veridiction (games of truth)
Domination	> power	> government
Individuals	> subjects	> self

Figure 1.1 Foucault's Displacements 1.

others, but whose relations are constitutive of one another" (from the first of his last lectures, cited in Flynn (2005, p. 262). As Foucault explained, in yet another rendition of his project: "What I tried to do from the beginning was to analyze the process of 'problematization'—which means: how and why certain things (behaviour, phenomena, processes) became a problem" (Foucault, 1983a). That is, he went on to say, he tried to show "that it was some real existent in the world which was the target of social regulation at a given moment". While he does not by any means exclude aspects of social context from his analysis he asserted that "a given problematization" is "an answer given by definite individuals". Prosaically then, in relation to my own interests, the history of education policies, is precisely, a history of problematizations of education, set within a broader social field. Problematization is both an object of study and a method/a research disposition in Foucault's work.

The remaining chapters map very loosely and heuristically onto specific aspects of Foucault's *displacements*. This provides a way of selecting among the many things that might be said, and as a way of indicating how Foucault can be used to rethink and rewrite the history of education policy. In nineteenth century education we can view education policy as emerging in relation to a *reluctant* but *necessary* state and a set of uneasy relationships between the state, the teacher and the parent. This is set within a distribution and redistribution of *responsibilities*. In the nineteenth century, in a whole myriad of ways, the state began to assume *responsibility* for its citizens. Specifically social policy was a response to the *urban* problem. That is, education policy is a very good example of Foucault's point that "Population comes to appear above all else to be the ultimate end of government" (Gordon et al., 1991, p. 100) as a resource, and schooling is a perfect example of what he called the "daemonic" coupling of the "city game" and the "shepherd-game" (Gordon et al., 1991, p. 8) with teachers as a "secular political pastorate". That is, the cross implication of care and management, discipline and regulation, which I address through a genealogy of *exclusions* and of *blood*. In thinking about education policy in this way we have to both materialize the school, as architecture and organization and attend to the schooled body, the ways in which schooling and policy are written onto the body. Chapter 3 traces these genealogies in four "moments" in the twenty-first century, and considers also the culpability of the sociology of education in perpetuating the history of educational divisions with its focus on the family as *responsible* for inequality. Chapter 4 examines the educational present through a concern with neo-liberalism, performativity and freedom and the "*responsibilitization*" of the neo-liberal subject.

Two further things need to be addressed before we can begin; two things referred to above but not yet properly explained—history and power. In relation to Foucault, both have been subject to enormous interest and to considerable abuse. As the title of this book signals power, or *power relations*, is a central concept in the analysis of education and education policy. Power relations are, as Foucault states, "everywhere". But the "everywhere" here is not a rhetorical flourish, it is fundamental to his re-articulation of the analytics of power and his challenge to traditional sociological conceptions of power. He presents power in the modern period—remember power itself has a history—as like a shifting and changing interactive network of social relations among and between individuals, groups, institutions and structures that are political, economic and personal. Power is not something that can be possessed, it is not tangible and it does not stand over and against something we might call freedom. Power operates in many different kinds of relationship, it is "always already there" (Foucault, 1980a, p. 141), we are never "outside it". However, that does not mean it is a cage, rather it is a constituent of, and in part constitutes our relationships, even so it does not "answer everything". We cannot be outside of power relations but we can change them. Power is not a mode of subjugation, or a general system of domination and indeed power is as much about what can be said and thought as what can be done—it is discursive. Power is not merely prohibitive it is productive, a lot of the time it "makes us up" rather than grinds us down. Power is sometimes an opportunity to be successful, fulfilled or loved. It is not always harmful. We are active within relations of power. Power is not then a structure but rather a complex arrangement of social forces that are exercised; it is a strategy, embedded in other kinds of relations. It is calculative but non-subjective. It has rationality separate from the individuals who enact it. The person "is the 'place' where power is enacted and the place where it is resisted" (Mills, 2003, p. 35). Discourse can be both an "instrument of power" and a "stumbling block" to it. Power is a multiplicity of intersecting and overlapping "force relations" of different kinds, that may be joined up or discontinuous, and are set within a "process of ceaseless struggles and transformations" (Foucault, 1981, pp. 92–93), relations are not static, but nonetheless, at some points in time may as a set of strategies form a "general design or institutional crystallization" that is "embodied in the state apparatus".

However, these force relations are "immanent" rather than general, they are "local and unstable" (p. 93) and operate inside other kinds of relations (economic, sexual, familial). The basic molecules of power relations, what Foucault calls the "microphysics of power" are individual choices, interactions and behaviours (tactics) that together produce more general social patterns (strategies)—hence his interest in details, rather than the end forms of power, in the mundane and meticulous, in small points of control and minute specifications, although given all of this it is never quite clear whether power might be "stored" within social institutions or roles. In this outline we can see a set of relationships between the theoretical and empirical analytics of power, between a way of conceptualizing power and a methodology, in the proper sense of the word, for its study; although Foucault commented that "relations of power are among the best hidden things in the social body" (Foucault, 1998, p. 119). His own empirical work on power was in the earlier studies *The Birth of the Clinic* and *Discipline and Punish* (Foucault, 1977a), and the more theoretical expositions came later in *The History of Sexuality*, etc. The methodology is a materiality of power, the power of bricks and mortar, of bodies and of social events—the diagnosis, the confession, the classroom question—all of which has been very attractive to feminists (see Sawicki, 1991) in particular, despite the absence of gender as a theme in Foucault's work. Despite the critics, there is also a clear recognition of the state in this, or as the effect of all this, "which consists in the codification of a whole number of power relations which render its functioning possible" (Foucault, 1988b, p. 122). This is the conception of the state, or at least the modern state, that is taken up in the following chapter. Foucault elaborated on some "specific features" of the modern state in his 1978–79 lecture series on *The Birth of Biopolitics* (2010a).

Foucault's insistence on the "relations of power" is related to his insistence that "resistance is never in a position of exteriority to power" (Foucault, 1981) and that "there cannot be relations of power unless the subjects are free" (1981, p. 12). Like power itself, resistance is also manifold and operates at a multiplicity of points in different forms, in many small acts and passing moments, with different purposes and possibilities—Foucault was particularly interested in popular uprisings and what he calls "anti-authority struggles" as "attacks" upon "a technique, a form of power" (Foucault, 1982, p. 212). This fits more generally with his interest in those positioned outside of mainstream society—the mad, abnormal, surreal and violent—"exiles and lepers" as he termed them; and as in the case of his examination of the confession of mass murderer Pierre Riviere (Foucault, 1975). Nonetheless, it would be valid to note that his theoretical interest in freedom in relation to power was much more evident in his later work than in his earlier work. Many readers find the earlier work on power conjuring up a bleak dystopian world of discourses and disciplines in which we are little else than manifestations of power relations, that these *are* "everything" as well as "everywhere". But, perhaps in apologist mode, we need to remember that Foucault was not, in his own terms, a theorist, nor did he seek to develop a general social theory (see Olssen, 2006, for an excellent account) rather he was engaged in developing "strategic knowledge" brick by brick. He said: "the question 'What is power' is obviously a theoretical question that would provide the answer to everything, which is just what I don't want to do" (Foucault, lecture 1973–74, p. 33).

As should be clear already, one of the primary facets of Foucault's "method" is the production of histories or genealogies. This follows logically from his rejection of essentialisms and universals. The histories are both a way of demonstrating uncertainty and contingency, and that absolutes are historical and are vehicles for the construction of an "ontology of the present". This is the work undertaken in *Discipline and Punish* and *The History of Sexuality*. Taking his lead from Nietzsche, Foucault's genealogy also consists of a refusal of continuities and of organizing principles to history, there is no "timeless and essential secret" (1984a, p. 78) to be uncovered by history, indeed this is an "adolescent quest" (p. 79) he says. Rather as Prado (1995, p. 34) puts it "history is only the painstaking tracking of complexity and disparity", indeed the focus in genealogies is on microparticulars or singularities—"minute deviations ... reversals ... errors ... false appraisals" (p. 36). Genealogical work:

> ... means making visible a singularity at places where there is a temptation to invoke a historical constant, an immediate anthropological trait, or an obviousness which imposes itself uniformly on all. To show that things "weren't as necessary as all that."
>
> (Foucault, 1991b, p. 76)

The body plays a key role in this, literally and metaphorically, "the body is the inscribed surface of events" and it "bears and manifests the effects of regulating discourses" (Foucault, 1984a, p. 82). The task of genealogy is to "expose a body totally imprinted by history" (p. 82). The focus on the body then does two things. It makes history visceral, a history of tortures, confinement and order, the acts of power of different sorts, violent and minute, exerted on the physical person. And it serves to displace the self and the subject. The subject becomes contingent, an historical production, not something prior to discourse and discipline, rather an effect of "a particular stage of forces"—what Foucault following Nietzsche calls "emergence". What seems "natural" or truthful or inevitable is in fact enabled by clashes of forces, everything has a history and has lowly beginnings. Genealogies are histories of things that are supposed to have no history. In particular, genealogy focuses on the histories of modalities of power. All of this announces a philosophical and epistemological rejection of key shibboleths of modern Western thought and what makes such thought possible, and seeks to invent a new vocabulary for history. This is frightening and threatening, this really is about thinking differently. It is an attempt to debunk traditional history, its procedures, presuppositions and philosophy of knowledge. It is Foucault's own act of usurpation, and he is attacking both what we theorize about and our theoretical tools. Practically speaking genealogical work involves "a vast accumulation of source material" and requires "relentless erudition" (1984a, pp. 76–77). The immediate problem is that neither is easy to live up to, and most examples of genealogical work involve understandable accommodations with "traditional" history and its methods—which will certainly also be the case here.

I am reluctant, and to a great extent ill-equipped, to undertake a proper philosophical discussion of genealogy and its Nietzschean bases, but we can turn to Prado (1995) and Mahon (1992) to do this. Rather, I want to highlight some key "practical" features of genealogy that may at least allow us to contemplate an attempt at *starting* a genealogy of education policy. The attention to genealogy as fundamental to Foucault's intellectual practice underlines the continuities and recurrences within his work from *Madness and Civilisation* to *The History of Sexuality*. Genealogy is the primary domain of analysis in Foucault's work, which derives from a "previous" one, archaeology, although they overlap (Prado, 1995). They are similar in that Foucault, through them, retells the histories of disciplines, institutions and practices drawing on excluded and hidden texts or voices, therefore troubling the hegemony of established histories. The task is to find out how a human being was envisaged in a particular period and the social practices that constituted this human being. This is not about demonstrating how limited or constrained or determined we are, but exactly the opposite, it is about showing the contingency and revocability of what and who we are and unmaking of solidity and inevitability, creating the possibilities for transgression. It is in this vein that Mendieta (2011) argues that genealogy offers us a "creative freedom that opens up horizons of being by challenging us ... to step over the limit". In relation to power Foucault was also interested in the "other side" of history—in "subjugated" and "disqualified" knowledges (Foucault, 1980b, p. 82). He says "Let us give the term genealogy to the union of erudite knowledge and local memories which allows us to establish a historical knowledge of struggles and to make use of this knowledge tactically today" (p. 83).

Here then are the tools from Foucault's toolbox on which I shall draw; here are some of my starting points and something of the position I will take in the rest of the book; here are some of the possibilities and impossibilities of doing Foucault; here are my reasons for wanting to read Foucault and for wanting to write a book with Foucault in the title; here are my excuses in advance for those occasions in what follows when I lapse back into "traditional" social science.

The following three chapters sketch and develop an argument, but they can be read in any order. Indeed, as I read the books proofs, Chapter 2 seems rather tortuous and in some ways might read more easily or more clearly after Chapter 3. In the most straightforward sense Chapter 2 seeks to establish a basis for recasting policy studies as a history of exclusions, it is a close engagement with some of Foucault's less well used lectures. Chapter 3 applies the analysis outlined in Chapter 2 to a set of case 'in the present'.

2

LET'S REWRITE THE HISTORY OF EDUCATION POLICY

Though Foucault himself never wrote an extended history of education, he could easily have. Education like the prison and sexuality, is fundamental in shaping modern western society and in its effects on subjects.

(Devine-Eller, 2004, p. 1)

I have come to the conclusion that there is no way of truly understanding what genealogy is about, other than by concentrating on a genealogy per se, analyzing it in its minor details, reaching the most remote points of its network, revealing the hidden micro-mechanisms of its operation, grasping the most delicate aspects of its theorisation. This is the first stage that inevitably leads to the adventure of writing one's own genealogy.

(Tamboukou, 2003, p. 140)

In this chapter and the next I will work on a set of "critical" and "effective" histories of education policy but ones that are not simply self-referential. That is to say, histories that are not "about" Foucault, but about "doing" genealogy as an exercise of "interpretive analytics". Effective history (*wirkliche Historie*) focuses on the interplay of knowledge and power, seeks to destabilize nature and the self and is divergent, incorporating marginalities and discontinuities. This will be a way of addressing "practical issues, necessities, and the limits of the present" (Dean, 1994, p. 20), starting from "questions posed in the present" (Foucault, 1988a, p. 262). These will be histories that have no determinist ascription of causality, but do have many recurrences and are embedded in "the endless repeated play of dominations" (Foucault, 1984b, p. 150)—that is, the advance of humanity from one domination to another. Doing policy history this way means avoiding the search for depth, and rather having a focus on the superficial, that is on details, on the nitty-gritty, but certainly not the trivial (Dreyfus & Rabinow, 1983). That is, a primary focus on practices rather than laws, on discourses rather then rhetorics, on techniques and procedures rather than structures. This will involve several *layers* of analysis—a set of interrelated genealogies and different readings of history—undertaken, by exposing them to scrutiny, to render certain taken-for-granted exercises of power "intolerable".

I approach this bearing in mind Samuel Beckett's entreaty: "Ever tried. Ever failed. No matter. Try Again. Fail again. **Fail better**"; but also Maria Tamboukou's point (2003, p. 9), that many of the philosophical and theoretical questions "that are raised by the use of genealogy, are more effectively worked out in the actual 'writing' of specific genealogies". What this will entail then is a set of starting points and some opening gambits and forays, "open dossiers" Foucault called them, rather than fully worked through examples. I will draw upon some of Foucault's lectures and on some bits of *Discipline and Punish* that do not seem to be very well attended to in most applications in educational analysis. I will also take Foucault's words to explore further some relations to which he only gestured in passing. These are passionate histories addressed to things than cannot be tolerated, but I realize also that they offer many opportunities for misunderstanding. The raw material for these analytics will be drawn mainly from England but I will be trying to establish a set of general principles of schooling. It is the method that is important.

In effect I will also be working on myself, trying to reposition or rewrite myself in relation to what sort of practice education policy analysis might be. This will involve interrupting or repositioning some of the commas in and exclusions from the analytical field of sociology of education (Troyna 1994) and groping towards a different kind of ethical practice. I will return to this effort in Chapter 4.

Ramshackle, Ugly and Smelly

> Under appalling conditions in our school the staff worked honestly but with no great hope. The building itself stood face on to one of the largest marshalling yards in the North. All day long the roar of a work-a-day world invaded the school hall, where each instructor, shouting in competition, taught up to sixty children massed together. From the logbook it is clear that rarely did a week pass with all teachers present. 'Miss F. or Mr. D. absent today—ulcerated throat' appears throughout with monotonous regularity.

Fortunately for the size of the classes, anything up to a quarter of the pupils would stay away too, perhaps in sympathy. One of our dominies, a frail young Scot, had, we thought, the disgusting habit of coughing into his handkerchief, then staring into it. We could not as yet spot the active consumptive looking anxiously for signs of hemorrhage.

His Majesty's inspector seemed permanently dissatisfied with us. These gentlemen we learned to recognise: they came in pairs like comedians, addressing us with some unction. Teachers feared them as they feared the Lord; scholars knew and enjoyed their terror. Many the looks of gratitude we, the bright boys, got for responding smartly to these god-like questioners.

(Roberts, *The Classic Slum,* 1973, Pelican Books, p. 134)

Late nineteenth century state education in England was a ramshackle affair, a hasty and reluctant construction based on and "filling in" the existing patchwork of religious and philanthropic schools that had "emerged less from the pens of legislators, theorists or reformers and far more from the material imperatives of discipline" (Deacon, 2006, p. 122). From 1870 the new state Board schools became a part of the burgeoning industrial landscape, factories of learning, based on a hit and miss method of mass production, often in inadequate buildings with few resources.[1] As Hunter (1996, p. 147) puts it "it is not educational principles that are central to the role of education systems but school premises". Many of these were "ugly" and smelly (McCulloch, 2011), they were an "improvised historical institution" (Hunter, 1996, p. 147). Nonetheless, they represented a new kind of state, a physical and empirical state, at the corner of the street, embodied in new kinds of state actors—teachers and head teachers and inspectors, who were also assembled into and represented a new form and modality of the state, the bureaucracy. This was enacted via new knowledges and skills, sciences of the mind and of the nature of the child, to produce a "pedagogical machine". "The pedagogic object of elementary education was to understand the nature of children and then develop their faculties to their fullest potential" (Tate, 1857). These schools were part of what Foucault describes as "a multiple network of diverse elements—walls, space, institutions, rules, discourse" (1979, p. 307). Their materiality is important in a number of ways, as we shall see. The school developed as a regional institution in a more general network of power, as part of the "geo-politics" of "the carceral city" (p. 307), part of a "strategic distribution of elements of different natures and levels" (p. 307), although the relationships between the institutions in this network— orphanages, hospitals, reformatories, prisons, "homes" and asylums (see Scull, 1979)—changed over time, as did the dis- tribution of knowledges across them and these knowledges and their bearers were sometimes in contest. That is, while on the one hand this network of institutions constituted a relay of "micro-powers", an "archipelago", "on the other they are not univocal; they define innumerable points of confrontation, focuses of instability …" (Foucault, 1979, p. 27).

School teachers were trained; they were experts, of a sort and "ethical exemplars", of a kind. They were trained to be "virtuous" rather than "over-educated" (Jones, 1990, p. 62). They were discursively positioned as both "modern" and "moral" (Larsen, 2011), as bastions against chaos and social disorder and as scientifically and philosophically engaged. They would bring the children of the urban masses under their "moral observation" (Donald, 1992). As with the asylum, the schools sought "to impose, in a universal form, a morality that will prevail from within upon those who were strangers to it"

(Foucault, 2001b, p. 246). Significantly the state began to take on responsibility for the training of teachers well before it took on responsibility for schools. The formation of teaching as a proto-profession, the limitation of its field and the definition of its object were implicated in a political structure and a moral practice at the centre of which is the establishment of "the learner" as a domain of knowledge (*savoir*) (see Popkewitz & Brennan, 1998). Foucault's three "aspects of experience"—truth, power and ethics—are very evident in relation to schooling and to the learner. Their organization within a field of knowledge—pedagogy, as an area of political intervention—compulsion and inspection and as an ethical position—forms of relation to oneself and to others, for example the teacher as class model. Each of these aspects were "affected by transformations in the other two" (Foucault, 1997a).

Teachers and learners were positioned within systems of inspection and comparison and "terror"—"payment by results" (Perryman, 2007), which as the name indicates, again like the factory, related funding to productivity, to output—a generic economic methodology of government. The judgments of the Inspectors were also embedded in the classificatory practices of the classroom as new types of learner, "bright" boys and their "failing" counterparts, were identified within the newly evolving techniques of pedagogy and assessment. New types of learner were being produced and created by the "humble modalities" of organization, compulsion and expertise in the school, "the bright" and also "the absent", who may be subject to very direct intervention. In 1880 schooling became compulsory for 6–10 year olds, and the "whippers in", later "education welfare officers", were another new state actor whose job was to get children off the streets and into the school, and to try to ensure that families took on the responsibility of sending their children to school. Parents were quickly recruited to and classified in relation to the ethics of compulsion. And yet in relation to all of this, some children were deemed "unassimilable" and were "educated" elsewhere (see below). As noted already, the new state schools were also part of a matrices of other buildings, bureaucracies and practices that constituted "the grid of power" in the nineteenth century city, including a nascent system of public health that had begun to identify diseases and their patterns, using the methods of statistics, epidemiology and the infrastructures of sanitation, to combat outbreaks of cholera, as well as hospitals, asylums and prisons. This is what Hunter (1996, p. 153) calls "an archipelago of calculative institutions" that were "assembled from the moral and material grab bag of western culture" (p. 147). Inside these institutions, "Technical social science began to take form within the context of administration" (Dreyfus & Rabinow, 1983, p. 134). Government, as the "political technology of the body" (Foucault, 1979, p. 26), was increasingly concerned with the minds and bodies of its populace and their well-being, as an indicator and facilitator of the well-being of the nation and its security. Schools via their own "arbitrary cruelties" were beginning to assume their intermediary socializing and civilizing role between family and work. Government and opportunity, capability and freedom were juxtaposed in the "positive liberty" of state schooling. As Robert Lowe, the Chancellor of the Exchequer, remarked following the passing of the 1867 Reform Act, "now we must educate our masters".

Anyone who can compare the demeanour of our young people at the present day with what it was five and twenty years ago must notice how roughness of manner has been smoothed away, how readily and intelligently they can answer a question, how the half-hostile suspicion with which they regarded a stranger has disappeared; how, in fact, they have become civilised.

(Report of HMI, 1895)

The state both extended its scope across the new landscape of the social and adopted new methods. "The watchword now became National Efficiency, a programme for redefining and extending the powers of the state through reforms in government, industry and social organisation, as well as education" (Donald, 1992, p. 27). The population as a resource had to be garnered and nurtured within "the mundane objectives of the administrative state—social order, economic prosperity, social welfare" (Hunter, 1996, p. 153). This was a new type of political rationality and practice which "no longer sought to achieve the good life nor merely to aid the prince, but to increase the scope of power for its own sake by bringing the bodies of the state's subjects under tighter discipline" (Dreyfus & Rabinow, 1983, p. 137)—making them "sober, healthy and competitive" (Jones & Ball, 1995, p. 68).

It is here then we can begin to (re)construct the problem of the history of the modern school and the history of contemporary education policy as a set of relations among games of truth and practices of power. Both as a series of shifts "jolts and surprises", and as the play of continuities or recurrences through the application of techniques of power and the deployment of forms of knowledge which "constantly carve out new objects" (Foucault, 2009, p. 79). Education policy in this sequence is a locus of activity in the myriad of mechanisms of security, which focus on the management of the population and its "naturalness", although marked by recurrences—productivity, blood, normality, classification/exclusion, and welfare—and their interplay. Here then we can begin to rewrite the history of education policy in two closely related ways, as a history of classifications and exclusions and as a history of blood. This is attempted below along and between three interrelated, vectors—"abnormality", "race" and social class. I will sketch out some of aspects of these histories in this chapter and take them a little further in the next. This is also very much, in the spirit of Foucault's work, a history of problematizations. Bearing in mind that problematization is "what has made possible the transformation of difficulties and obstacles of a practice into a general problem for which one proposes diverse practical solutions ... it defines the elements that will constitute what the different solutions attempt to respond to" (Foucault, 1984 [1997], p. 5).

A History of Classifications

Now, if we are to take these genealogical beginnings of a history of education policy further, two interruptions need to be made. First, there are two techniques and two politics involved here, *disciplinary* and *regulatory*, and we need to attend to both, and to their relations. Discipline is anatomo-politics, and regulation is biopolitics. These are two forms or levels of power which intertwine with the aim of the management of the population. Disciplinary power, which focuses on the individual body and is concerned with the "disciplinary technology of individual dressage" (Stoler, 1995, p. 82) and regulatory power, which is concerned with the life of the body of the species and is "globalising" rather than individualizing. This latter is the "bio-regulation of the state", and is concerned with the internal dangers to society at large (Stoler, 1995, p. 82). Second, in thinking about what our history consists of, it is not the school or the state on which we should focus our attention, but rather on the technologies that make up the school as an institution, that constitute its functioning and effects, and the form and methods of the state. As Tamboukou (2003, p. 11) emphasizes "the more the analysis breaks down practices, then easier it becomes to find out more about their interrelation". So let us start again with the anonymous and functional power of discipline, "the regime of disciplinary power as effect and object of power, as effect and object of knowledge" (Foucault, 1979, p. 192). That is, a *genealogy of classifications*, or perhaps more precisely a genealogy of nor-mation and normalization.

We can do this by drawing from one particular lecture, that was given by Foucault at the College de France on January 25, 1978 in the series *Security, Territory, Population*. He began the lecture by explaining that he intended to move his focus from "mechanisms of discipline" to "apparatuses of security" and to emphasize the distinction between them. He said, he wanted to "put a stop to repeated invocations of the master and the monotonous assertion of power" (Foucault, 2009, pp. 55–56). In this lecture Foucault summarized his view of discipline as "very roughly and schematically things that have been said a thousand times" (p. 56). Discipline he said "normalises" and "of course analyzes and breaks down; it breaks down individuals, places, time, movements, actions and operations. It breaks them down into components such that they can be seen, on the one hand, and modified on the other" (p. 56). We could take the classroom as a paradigm of discipline in these senses. It is fundamentally organized in these terms. Learners are "seen" and "modified" and "broken down", by age and sometimes by gender, by ability, by "need", in relation to talents and other forms of specialty or abnormality. Schools are broken down into houses, the school day into a timetable and a curriculum (a serial space of serial knowledges) and into specialist locations; pupil movements are broken down within and into lessons, they are allocated to seats, organized onto tables or in rows, labelled, tested, measured and calculated by the techniques of examination. Literacy and writing, grading and examination, were developed as forms of discipline and differentiation, locating learners within a "grammocentric world" in which human abilities could be calculated and compared (Hoskin, 1990). The discipline of writing was both a means of measuring and recording the learner—"power introduced individuality into the field of observation, but power fixes that objectivity individual in the field of writing" (Dreyfus & Rabinow, 1983, p. 159). The new technologies of measurement and examination quickly gave rise to a proliferation of "scholastic accountancy", lodged in various "ignoble archives" (Foucault, 1979, p. 191)—within which children were measured (literally), filed (in both senses) and photographed (see Humphries & Gordon, 1992). As Donald (1992, p. 31) says: "there was nothing covert or mysterious about these techniques. They were built into the very structure and routine of the schools".

Schooling was built (literally again) on the contradictory bases of uniformity and individuality, a collectivist vision mediated within the methodologies of division and differentiation. Indeed, the very idea of the school, its materiality, its imaginary, its articulation within policy and theory came to be centered on and enacted in terms of a machinery of differentiation and classification, and concomitantly of exclusion (c.f. Bennett, 1995). Slee (2011, p. 42) says, exclusion is "an institutional feature or part of the grammar of schooling". The school became in many respects an expression of humanity and a demarcation of the limits to humanity—who was and was not educable, of value, worth investing in. This is what Baker (1998, p. 138) calls the "limits of normal childhood", framed then and now by pedagogical and psychological categories; "feeble-minded", "backward", "at risk" "ready to learn", "ADHD", "emotionally disturbed", "learning disabled", a "zoology of sub-species" (Oksala, 2007, p. 50), formed within the practices and knowledges of "intelligence", orderliness, speed of recall, articulated with race and class, to produce a "space of otherness reserved for children already othered through a variety of discourses" (Baker, 1998, p. 138). The power of discipline is "one of analysis" (Foucault, 1979, p. 197) to locate and separate, that is "power organises an analytic space" (p. 143) a "cellular space" and a "therapeutic space" (p. 144), a space of "precision" (p. 143) and distribution. Here power produces reality as a domain of objects articulated in specific rituals of truth—measurement.

In late nineteenth century England learner "abilities" and teacher competencies were organized and normalized in relation to the appropriately named Standards, with all its moral connotations. Foucault says the school became in the nineteenth century an "apparatus of uninterrupted examination" (1979, p. 186), the examination is a mechanism of simultaneous evaluation and comparison "woven into [the school] through a constantly repeated ritual of power" (p. 186). The learner is made visible, but power is rendered invisible, and the learner sees only the tasks and the tests which they must undertake. The Standards separated skills out into simple, individually analyzable competencies, "allowing for the ranking of individuals and the assignment of individual exercises for improvement" (Devine-Eller, 2004, p. 6). This, in turn, produced a temporal ordering of subjects (in all senses) in relation to one another (Foucault, 1979, p. 159), within which some are "ahead" and others "behind", some remediable and others not. In this way "disciplinary time … was gradually imposed on pedagogical practice" (p. 159) and "a pedagogical hierarchy was created, dividing students up into more and more finely-differentiated units" (Devine-Eller, 2004, p. 7). A space was created within which over time both "developmental" and cognitive psychologies could flourish and clash. In other words, teaching and the curriculum began to be organized, and thus learners categorized, in relation to what Bernstein (1990) called "pacing and sequencing", or what Foucault called "optimal sequences and coordinations" (2009, p. 57), based on the "seriation" of time (Foucault, 1979, p. 160) and "the possibility of a detailed control and regular intervention (of differentiation, correction, punishment, elimination)" (p. 160). Intervention, together with decisions related to pacing and sequencing also produced a new space for practical expertise and over time for theory and for pedagogy and for anti-pedagogy—remedial education, a particular sub-field of pastoral and disciplinary expertise.

The techniques and humble procedures of pedagogical power are minute and fussy and unobtrusive and "For Foucault, then, time is both 'evolutive' and 'cumulative', stable, linear, and oriented towards a terminal point, but also serial and progressive" (Devine-Eller, 2004, p. 7). The "tyranny of the devil's mill", the clock, which facilitated the reform of factory work and its relation to wages (Foucault 2006a), was also a basic organizing principle of the school. Rhythms, repetitions and cycles, produced an "anatomo-chronological schema" for the school firmly rooted in the modern *episteme*.

> The present is always seen to be a matter of progress in relation to time passed and the time remaining measured against these fixed reference points. Consciousness in the present is tied to a fixed horizon of the future, time is limited but can be saved, made up and used wisely. The experience of the activity, the task, is subordinate to the "pace" set by the teacher [in relation to the examination, the standard, the level]. Class lessons are frequently punctuated by urgent enquiries from the teacher as to "who has not finished?" "How many of you have not got on to question 5?" "Hurry up you three the rest of us are waiting."

(Ball, Hull et al., 1984, pp. 41–42)

Time also engenders a whole set of micro-penalties, for lateness, absence, interruption, as part of a "punishable, punishing universality" (Foucault, 1979, p. 178) which also encompassed laziness, insolence, and lack of cleanliness. Punishments in schools included both the "spectacle" of "monarchical practices"—the cane, the slipper, the taws—and increasingly over time reformatory and therapeutic practices. The point was "not to punish less but to punish better" (p. 76). The school quickly developed as a meticulous nexus of disciplines of formal, fussy, mundane and repetitive actions and operations on the learner, an "analytical-practical grid" (pp. 56–57) of perception and modification, or what Bernstein called "repair". Learners are fixed by measurement but also subject to continual interventions which aim to change and move them in relation to markers of "development". This is related to the second characteristic of discipline identified by Foucault, which is that "discipline classifies the component thus identified according to definite objectives" (p. 57) and as an example asks "What children are capable of obtaining a particular result?" (p. 57). What this points out is one of the organizing principles of schooling, that of *grouping by performance*, in terms of difference and similarity—the erasure of difference. *Schools systems, with few exceptions are rooted in a history of classifications and differentiations, in particular those that are articulated by performance, which is taken to be an indicator of something deeper—ability.* Grouping and differentiation are aspects of the construction of whole school systems and finite distinctions enacted in classroom on a daily basis. The arts and competencies of teaching are in good part defined by these acts and techniques of classification.

Central to processes of *classification* Foucault argues is *normalization,* "the primary and fundamental character of the norm" (p. 57), as a standard that unifies practice. In school, normalization is most evident and familiar as a distribution of ability and as a concomitant typology of rank positions. In a number of ways we find *ability*, as an effect or articulation of the norm, produced at the heart of schooling, the very point at which teaching could articulate a form of knowledge which related pedagogy to population, and classroom practice to a general theory of management, distribution and entitlement. Measures (standards), methods (examination), techniques of analysis (statistics) which latterly attached themselves to knowledge (psychology) provided a technical repertoire for the classification of learners and the population as a whole. That is, a nexus of power/knowledge and a human science, which writes the history of education policy, as a record, a file, a rank, an individuality directly onto that bit of the body, we call the mind. Power/knowledge relations operate here to produce the phenomenon to which they are addressed—the individual learner. The idea of the individual is not "the vis-à-vis of power; it is … one of its prime effects" (Foucault, 1980a, p. 98). The school developed a conception of the learner within the framework of liberal possessive individualism "in the condition of the individual as essentially the proprietor of his (or presumably her) own person and capacities" (Olssen, 1993, pp. 163–164). Increasingly schooling was infused by a psychology fixated with the individual and individual difference, both normatization and pathologization, and realized within a set of assessing, diagnostic, prognostic and normative practices. The emergence of the modern individual is seen here as the object of both political and scientific concern.

Also here a subtle shift is signalled, concomitant with the development of the human sciences and what Rose (1999) calls the *psy-sciences*, from schooling as primarily a set of routines of habit and manner, to schooling as the certification and channeling of abilities. The "learner" emerged as a subject of pedagogy in relation to the norm, in an orthogonal relationship of distributions across the population and over time—intelligence and cognitive development. The field of educational psychology, which emerged as a branch of psychology in the late nineteenth century, became "a central force in the everyday lives of ordinary people and a central institutional base from which technical, social and educational problems were tackled within specialist university departments of education" (Olssen, 1993, p. 155).

"The school became the place for elaboration for pedagogy … the age of the 'examining school' marks the beginnings of a pedagogy that functions as a science" (Foucault, 1979, p. 187). On the one hand, increasingly, the human sciences enabled modern power to circulate through finer channels.

They colonized and operated the institutions of modern power in particular ways, through their knowledges and technologies, and those institutions, like the school and the teacher, made certain forms of knowledge possible, indeed necessary. On the other, they structured ways of knowing and exercising power that brought into existence esoteric regimes of power/knowledge. We can recognize these technologies and knowledges at work in the contemporary school, as evidence of their effectiveness and continuing anonymous necessity, embedded in a broader complex of discourses and practices through which childhood and the pupil are "made up", and normalized, in what MacNaughton (2005, p. 30) calls "officially sanctioned developmental truths of the child". Such relations of power/knowledge, repeated in many other institutional settings, make the state possible, in the modern sense, they constitute it as a set of mechanisms, a dispositif ("the coupling of a set of practices and a regime of truth" [Foucault, 2010a, p. 18], to form an apparatus) in relation to the problem of population. "The government, particularly the administrative apparatus, needed knowledge that was concrete, specific and measurable in order to operate effectively" (Dreyfus & Rabinow, 1983, p. 137). The state is a set of techniques and relationships, commandeered from elsewhere and generalized, totalized, in all their cumbersome and "brute efficacy" (Deacon, 2006, p. 131).

So far this is a fairly familiar and orthodox application of Foucault's analytics to the emergence of the state school, and the dissolution of "multiplicities" into individual bodies. However, it is a one-sided account in as much that it attends to a set of *disciplinary* rather than *regulatory* techniques. It focuses almost entirely on "the disciplinary technology of labor" (Foucault, 2004a, p. 242) to the neglect of what Foucault called "natalist policy" (p. 243), or to "an anatomo-politics of the human body" (p. 243), as opposed to the biopolitics of the human race, concerned with "birthrate, longevity, public health, housing and migration" (Foucault, 1981, p. 140). Yet, the school is one of those places where the body and population meet, where ability confronts degeneracy, where the norm produces abnormality. The norm is the point of concatenation—"normalisation becomes one of the great instruments of power at the end of the classical age" (Foucault, 1979, p. 184). Foucault writes that "there is one element that will circulate between the disciplinary and the regulatory" and which will "make it possible to control both the disciplinary order of the body and the aleatory events that occur in the biological multiplicity" (p. 253)—that is the norm. This intersection is what he called "a normalising society" within which "power took possession of life" (p. 253). The two poles, anatomo-politics and biopolitics, he says were "linked together by a whole cluster of relations" (Foucault, 1980a, p. 139), which here include: the teacher, the test, grouping by ability, the educational psychologist, special schooling, race and class. Schooling is one point on the "crossroads where that power over, and invested in, individual bodies and populations would converge in technologies of discipline and regularization" (Stoler, 1995, p. 83). So let us start again at a slightly different point and look at the norm and the state, and power and the population in slightly different way—through a genealogy of blood.

Urban Education and the History of Blood

There are already signaled here various related ways in which we might begin to rethink the history of schooling and education policy in the present—that is as a history of classifications or exclusions, of normalizations, of modifications (therapy/repair), of time perhaps, or indeed of expertise/ knowledge. These can also be interpolated in more general terms as histories of subjects (teachers and learners and "others") and of practices (examination, grouping pedagogy), and of discourses (psychology, heredity, abnormality). However, I want to try to tie some of these genealogical starting points together and to write another history of education policy, *a history of blood*. That is, a history of the present, a "fictional" history (Foucault, 1992, p. 193) which puts education, in its various manifestations at the centre of the problem of *the urban* and the concomitant problem of the population. A history which puts the "excluded", the educational "other"—racism and disability—at the centre of the history of education policy. A history which puts marginality and exclusion "at the heart" of the discipline of schooling (Foucault, 1979, p. 301). Here I draw on two of Foucault's lecture series *Security, Territory, Population* (1977–1978) and *Society Must be Defended* (1976) and in particular on part of one lecture in the latter series. At times I am going to work closely with Foucault's text and terminology, particularly his use of the term "race". The argument is precise but also shocking and complex and I want to be as clear as I can.

In 1841 England became the first urban society. The census that year—and the census itself is a technique of relevance here—found more people living in towns and cities than in the countryside. In Victorian society the city was a focus of wonder and dread, of social opportunity and social problems. The city—London, Manchester, Liverpool and Bristol, for example—was also the centre of the Empire.

A node in increasingly diverse and complex global flows of populations and relations of power. Multiple migrations, national and international, were producing a new kind of urban population that was both the key to economic prosperity and a threat to moral and social order, a population, strange and dangerous and uncivilized, that needed to be governed in new ways.

> In these pages I propose to record the results of a journey with pen and pencil into a region, which lies at our own doors—into a dark continent that is within easy walking distance of the General Post Office. This continent will, I hope, be found as interesting as any of those newly-explored lands which engage the attention of the Royal Geographical Society—the wild races who inhabit will, I trust, gain public sympathy as easily as those savage tribes for whose benefit the Missionary Societies never cease to appeal for funds.
>
> (*How the Poor Live,* by George R. Sims, 1883,
> Preface, Chapter 1, p. 5)

In the messy proximities of the burgeoning city, morality, poverty, social order, prosperity and social reform—health, education and sanitation—were tightly tied together in Victorian fears and concerns of contagion both social and moral. As Foucault put it "The town as market is also the town as the place of revolt; the town as center of diseases is the town as the site of miasmas and death" (2009, pp. 63–64). Robert Kay-Shuttleworth (a Doctor, Poor Law Commissioner, a founder member of the Manchester Statistical Society and Secretary to The Committee of the Privy Council on Education [1839–1849]—a paradigm of the new state actor) wrote of "the moral influence of the immigrants of semi-barbarous masses is prejudicial, by example, and personal intercourse, to the habits of the population with which they mingle" (Kay-Shuttleworth, 1862, pp. 151–152). Lord Macaulay in his 1874 speech before the House of Commons defended the state's responsibility to educate England's poor by comparing ignorance, spread through the lower classes, to "'a leprosy, or some other fearful disease' (House of Commons, 1847, p. 1008 cited in Larsen, 2011)" (cited in Larsen, 2011, p. 55). Larsen notes that "poverty was considered a sort of moral contamination transmitted through the parent" (p. 55) and that immoral habits were associated in particular with the urban Irish immigrant population. These concerns contributed to a "discourse of moral crisis … constituted by the fears, worries, anxieties and insecurities that middle-class Victorians felt towards the poor, labouring and immigrant populations" (p. 53). Thus, Foucault says: "The town posed new and specific economic and political problems of government technique" (Foucault, 2009, p. 64) and that in response a "very complex technology of securities appeared" (p. 64), of which the school became a key element; a particular site in which cleanliness, order and productivity could be addressed. Government was no longer simply a matter of defending boundaries and controlling territory, it became increasingly one of managing flows and resources—flows of populations, money, goods and diseases—and the production of productivity and docility. The problem "is no longer that of fixing and demarcating territory, but of allowing circulations to take place, of controlling them, sifting the good and bad, ensuring that things are always in movement, constantly moving around, continually going from one point to another, but in such a way that the inherent dangers of this circulation are cancelled out" (p. 65).

This is a shift, as Foucault referred to it, from Territory to Security. He looked at scarcity, town planning, the management of epidemics as examples of such problems and responses to them, and he considers in particular the role of statistics, which are articulated in a set of "new notions" in their field of application—"case, risk, danger and crisis" (Foucault 2009, p. 61), which were for the first time articulated in terms of "normal" distributions or "distributions of normality". He goes on to say "they are all linked to the phenomenon of the town itself" (p. 63). The population comes to be "considered as a set of processes to be managed at the level and on the basis of what is natural ..." (p. 70). The population becomes "a sort of technical–political object of management and government" (p. 70)—this is what in the lectures of the following year (1978–79) Foucault called *The Birth of Biopolitics*—that is, a regime of governmental reason within which economic truth is central (2010a, p. 22). The school became one tactical locus for the management of urban populations. From the nineteenth century on, certainly in Europe and many places elsewhere, the history of education policy is the history of urban education.

Naturalness—the biological, the organism—is a fundamental "knowing empiricity" (Foucault, 1970a, p. 250) in the modern *episteme*, as Foucault outlines in *The Order of Things*. Biology, the science of life, is one of the three "great hidden forces" (p. 251), alongside linguistics and economics (labour), which were to produce a whole new set of objects and methods of knowledge—the human sciences, the sciences of life—in the late eighteenth and nineteenth centuries. Biology, nature, is a key facet of the genealogy of education policy and the history of the educational present. This *naturalness, that which is natural,* appears in different ways. First, in the ways in which the population depends on a complex of variables, which means its management always eludes the sovereign–subject relationship, rather the naturalness "identified in the fact of population is constantly accessible to agents and techniques of transformation, on condition that these agents and techniques are at once enlightened, reflected, analytical, calculated and calculating" (Foucault, 2009, p. 71). The teacher is one such agent. The school is a cluster of such techniques. As signaled already, measurement, comparison and examination, numbers of many sorts, are embedded in and serve these techniques to produce domination and responsibilization and construct "calculating selves" and "centres of calculation". The second naturalness of population is that of desire or self-interest and thus the "idea of the management of populations on the basis of the naturalness of their desire"—that is, the production of a collective or general interest. Third, naturalness, rests in the discovery of the population as a set of constants and regularities—patterns of "behaviour"—distributions. "The population thus emerged as the bearer of an array of conducts and capacities that had been rendered problematic through the application of statistically determined norms and standards of living" (Hunter, 1996, p. 154). The techniques and rationalities of government, which were developed in the nineteenth century, are then "absolutely linked to the population" (Foucault, 2009, p. 76) and Foucault argues "the series, mechanisms of security—population—government and the opening up of the field that we call politics, should be analysed" (p. 76). According to Foucault, the modern state exercises its power, and governs, through the administration of life; it is preoccupied with life itself, rather than death. In these terms, as Bauman (1991, p. 39) says "Nature came to mean something to be subordinated to human will and reason". In the fourth lecture in the series *Security, Territory, Population*, Foucault named this new form of government "governmentality", what he calls a "singular generality"[2], and refers to "the governmentalisation" of the state (2009, p. 109) which, he goes on to say, ensures the survival of and defines the limits of the state[3]. Governmentality is a conceptual architecture of the modern liberal state and all its strategies, techniques and procedures as they act upon the human body and social behaviour through the many and varied capillaries of power.

Let us look at this point carefully. Importantly, the techniques of biopower do "not simply do away with the disciplinary technique, because it exists at a different level, on a different scale, and because it has a different bearing area, and makes use of very different instruments" (Foucault, 2004a, p. 242). Biopower relates not to "man as body" (the body-organism-discipline-institutions series, p. 250), but "man-as-living being" (the population-biological processes-regulatory mechanisms-state series, p. 250). The regulatory (biopower) and the disciplinary operate at different levels, what we might roughly call policy and practice, but which are closely inter-related at many points. Together regulation and discipline cover "the whole surface that lies between the organic and the biological" (p. 253). But crucially, Foucault argues that "the one element that will circulate between the disciplinary and the population alike" (p. 252) is the norm and all its paraphernalia. In particular, the "normal curve had within it deep assumptions of unity by which individuals could be compared on the same conceptual space to the entire population" a "regime of truth" from which "it has been almost impossible for any individual to escape" (Olssen, 1993, p. 165). The norm, and its intertwined moral and statistical applications, provided a scientific basis for the measurement and judgment "double", a "grid of intelligibility" within which individuals could be categorized and compared in relation to one another, and in relation to the national interest, and the management of the population as a resource. In particular, this form of government was to become increasingly concerned with the "dangers within", and their eradication—*that is eugenics* (Selden, 1999). The species, the population needed to be "fit"— in a moral, economic and biological sense and "One corollary of these anxieties about the 'fitness' of the population during the last decades of the century was the aspiration to breed—and educate—an 'imperial race'" (Donald, 1992, p. 27). As Foucault explained "the more inferior species disappear, the more abnormal individuals are eliminated, the less degenerates there are in the species, the more I—as individual, and as species—will live, be strong and vigorous and able to proliferate" (2004a, p. 265). Closely intertwined with *degeneracy* and resting on the same discursive bases is *abnormality*. Crucially in all of this, in assuming responsibility over the power of life, the state also assumes the "right to kill", in the interests of life—a thanatopolitics. Put succinctly: "Modern man is an animal whose politics places his existence in question" (Foucault, 1976 [1988], p. 143). Foucault goes on: "It is, I think, at this point that racism intervenes" (Foucault, 2004a, p. 254), racism long existed but "functioned elsewhere" as he put it. Racism is not new, but this is what he calls "new racism"[4]. "Once the state functions in the biopower mode, racism alone can justify the murderous function of the state" (p. 256). *Foucault is using the term racism here in a very particular and specific sense.*

That which links abnormality, degeneracy and racism is blood, represented both in the genetic composition of individuals and the health of the social body—that is, the national gene pool. Discipline and regulation are organized in relation to individuals and the population respectively through a "epistemology of order" (Shein, 2004, p. 9), a set of distinctions and classifications which, "fragments" the "biological continuum" as Foucault puts it, into categories, types and "races" which both identifies potential "enemies" to the health of the population and at the same times creates a norm—or rather a set of intersecting norms: able-bodiedness, masculinity, heterosexuality, and whiteness. "The norm is what can be applied to both the body that desires discipline, as well as to the population that desires regularization" (Foucault 2004a). Again, this draws upon and contributes to the development of social statistics and statistical techniques, which provided a language and set of concepts which served to distribute a population along the lines of a curve, that defines population norms and desirable traits, and creates a system of "normalisation" and not simply "normation" (c.f. *The Bell Curve* [Hernstein & Murray, 1994])[5]. Here, the "animalisation of man" and the holocaust makes its historical appearance (Dreyfus & Rabinow, 1983, p. 138).

As indicated, and as is often the case, Foucault is using the terms *racism* and *new racism* to refer much more generally to the "scientific" identification of genetic groups or classes or categories, that, as he says, establish divisions within the species, in relation to the norm, which then become the focus of scientific, political, ethical practices—subject to regulation. The divisions or "*breaks*" within the species is key here. For Foucault, the specificity of modern racism is not "bound up" with ideologies but is "bound up" with the techniques of power and here we see the link "between nineteenth century biological theory and the discourse of power" (2004a, p. 256). Darwinism plays a pivotal role here as "a set, a bundle, of notions" (p. 256) that provided "a real way of thinking about the relations between colonisation, the necessity of wars, criminality, the phenomena of madness and mental illness, the history of societies with their different classes and so on" (p. 257). A set of specialized and generalized interrelations between biological knowledge and modern power were established and this is the landscape of policy I want to adumbrate in relation to education.

This "new racism", in Foucault's sense, is "a break in the domain of life that is under power's control: the break between what must live and what must die" (Foucault, 2004a, p. 254), that is between the good and the inferior. It is a "biological caesura", which sub-divides the species and provides and accounts for the elimination (and/or exclusion) of the inferior, degenerate and abnormal, the "enemies" of population, for the benefit of all, it "is something that will make life in general healthier: healthier and purer" (p. 255). There is a double classification of the population; a multiple "breaking down" that is made possible by statistics and made moral by eugenics. That is to say, in the nineteenth century the knowledges and practices of medicine and Darwinism and penal theory together began to develop methods for identifying, isolating and "normalising" "abnormal" and "dangerous" individuals and social groups based on a combination of psychiatry, psychology and "knowledge of heredity"[6]. These new knowledges combine to provide a form of "social defense" against "abnormals". This involved the elimination of "biological dangers" and "the strengthening of the species". The responsibility for social defense was located in the state and its technologies of power, and "racism becomes a tool of the modern state" (Shein, 2004, p. 7). Foucault goes onto assert that in the twentieth century this "new" racism was linked by Nazism to "ethnic racism", his term for phenotypical racism. As Bauman argues Nazi policies of racial hygiene were the ultimate logic of rationality and order but racial hygiene, as he points out, had by 1932, "become a scientific orthodoxy in the German medical community" (1991, p. 41; Cornwell, 2004). Foucault goes further to argue that in relation to the new technologies of the "normalising state" racism is crucial in as much that it "represents the condition under which it is possible to exercise the right to kill" (Foucault, 2004a, p. 254). "Genocide", he says starkly, "is the dream of modern politics" (Foucault, 1981, p. 137), and goes on to say that "We should not be surprised that German psychiatry functioned so spontaneously with Nazism" (Foucault, 2004a, p. 317).

So where does this get us in rewriting the history of education policy? What I am suggesting is that the particular combination of truth and power adumbrated above, represented in particular in the sciences of intelligence, constituted the historical conditions of modern education, in the context of particular political and economic necessities, and that these conditions, this combination, remain as the foundations of education in the present. This is a moral–scientific nexus which articulates the body and history and within which the educated/uneducable body and its mind—its individuality— are imprinted with a history of categories and breaks, of race and abnormality. This is also a history of struggles—in relation to class, race, gender and ability (in all its senses) in particular—and a differentiation of values (although I do not have the space to attend to these here). This history is written into the mundane mechanisms and modes of thought of contemporary schooling. School is one of those "places where what is said and what is done, rules imposed and reasons given, the planned and the taken for granted, meet and inter-connect" (Defert & Ewald, 2001, pp. 102–103). This is *classification* "writ large" and small in institutional and classroom practices of ranking, division and exclusion, which are articulated by and in relation to the fragmentation of the species—an increasingly complex and interdependent relationship between "intelligence", race and abnormality, produced, legitimated and managed by the psychology of normality and of intelligence, most obviously in eugenics. We can begin to see in this history some very particular ways in which education in the nineteenth century became one point of intersection between discipline and regulation, between the individual and the social body, between individualizing and totalizing which in most respects remains in place today. From the nineteenth century on the history of education policy in England and elsewhere became the history of race and racism, in Foucault's sense. This is quintessentially a history of normality and of blood (genes/heredity) or we might think of this an aspect of what Foucault called "the political history of the body" (Foucault, 2003, p. 214)[7].

The interrelationships of science, language, professionalism, institutions, law and mundane institutional practices on the one hand, and health and education policy on the other were realized in a set of shifting categories, divisions, crises and exclusions which were enacted upon vulnerable bodies during the nineteenth and twentieth centuries (see Box 2.1

Box 2.1. **Some examples of "breaks", divisions and exclusions in relation to abnormality.**

1845 Lunacy Act—administered by Commissioners in Lunacy. It made no clear distinction between learning disability and mental illness stating that "Lunatic" shall mean insane person or any person being idiot or lunatic or of unsound mind.'

1847 The Charity for the Asylum of Idiots—established in London.

1850s and 1860s The Charity for the Asylum of Idiots gave impetus and support to the establishment of 4 regional *voluntary* large scale asylums for "idiots" in England: the Northern Counties (i.e. The Royal Albert); Eastern Counties Idiot Asylum (Colchester); Western Counties Asylum (Starcross, near Exeter); and Midland Counties Asylum (Staffordshire).

1867 Maudsley publishes *Psychology and Pathology of the Mind.*

1886 Idiots Act. For the first time legislation dealing with the educational needs of those with learning disability. It made a clear distinction between lunatics on one hand and "idiots" and "imbeciles" on the other.

1889 Education Departmental committee report on *The Education of Defective and Epileptic Children*

1890 Lunacy Act, which like its 1845 predecessor again muddied distinctions between learning disability and mental illness.

1907 Formation of Eugenics Education Society; prominent members included John Maynard Keynes, William Beveridge, Richard Titmuss and Marie Stopes.

1908 Report of Royal Commission on Care and Control of the Feeble-Minded

1908 Tredgold 1st edition of *Mental Deficiency, which* was the main reference text (with revisions) for the next 50 years in nurse training.

The report of a Royal Commission, published as the Radnor Report, was the main influence on the 1913 Mental Deficiency Act.

1913 Mental Deficiency Act. Use of terms "idiot", "imbecile", "feeble-minded" and "moral imbecile". In particular this influential Act made it possible to institutionalise women with illegitimate children who were receiving poor relief.

1910 Mary Dendy publishes *The Problem of the Feeble-Minded*
Campaign for Voluntary Sterilisation
Eugenics Movement at its height

1932 In response to pressure from the Eugenics Society the UK Minister of Health established a government committee (the Brock Committee) to report on the possibility of the enforced sterilisation of the "feeble minded" to address the problem of uneven reproduction across the social classes (see Chapter 3).

1934 Brock Report recommends voluntary sterilization

1934: Alva and Gunnar Myrdal's *Crisis of the Population* published

1937 Cyril Burt's *The Backward Child* published and the Queensland Backward Persons Act passed

1938 The Queensland Mental Hygiene Act passed

1938 Lionel Penrose published the "Colchester Report" (a clinical and genetic study of 1280 cases of Mental Defect)

1954–7 Royal Commission on the Law Relating to Mental Illness and Mental Deficiency (under Lord Percy). National Association of Parents of Backward Children gave evidence to Royal Commission

1955 Guild of Teachers of Backward Children founded
"Subnormal" and "severely subnormal" terms used in 1959 Act

1956 Tizard and O'Connor's *The Social Problem of Mental Deficiency* published

1970 Education (Handicapped Children) Act made education universal (See Chapter 3). for some examples).

Here there is an uneasy shifting mix between remnants of the "great confinement" of the seventeenth century, the "natural abode" (Foucault, 2001b, p. 36) of "handicap", and the management and classifications of the modern population as deserving and undeserving, productive and unproductive *resources*. There are elements of both remediation and *residualization*, and attempts to make "inmates" productive.

So from the mid-nineteenth century, social, health and education policy were focused on the problem of the population, population as a resource for the state to manage the achievement of productivity and docility. This is set over and against the "threats" and risks posed by mobility, migration and degeneracy, that is, "enemies who have to be done away with" (Foucault, 2004a, p. 256). These were "not adversaries" in the political sense of the term; they are "threats to the population". This is "the menace of the other within", to quote Armstrong (2003). The production and management of a "modern" population is articulated in an interplay between the strategies of biologism, normalization, distribution (in various senses), classification and exclusion, and the institutional tactics of schooling, public health, medicine, penality, sexuality, etc.—specific sites of "the rituals of power" and for "ceremonies of objectification". The "abnormal" human subject became an object-of-knowledge of the discourses of human and empirical sciences such as psychiatry, psychology, medicine and criminology and in the deployment of these psy-sciences fears were explained and managed.

Here in a particular way we see Foucault's point about racism and the management of life and death. The execution or banishment of "anomalies" it was argued, makes the population stronger. The "specificity of modern racism" is as a technique of power but in "juxtaposition" with "sovereign power"—"blood was a reality with a symbolic function" (Foucault, 2004a, p. 147). Drawing from the example of lepers in the Middle Ages Foucault speaks of "practices of exclusion" or "marginalisation" and says "I think we still describe the way in which power is exercised over the mad, criminals, deviants, children, and the poor in these terms … mechanisms and effects of exclusion, disqualification, exile, rejection, deprivation, refusal, and incomprehension" (Foucault, 2003, pp. 43–44). There is a curious and convoluted but very real interplay here between classification and exclusion. There is a double logic. I take entirely Armstrong's point that "Modernity was not, and logically could not be, about exclusion" (2003, p. 10) but rather about incorporation. Nonetheless, modern and previous logics and practices are intertwined here to produce internal exclusions and forms of disenfranchizement, for those defined on or beyond the limits of normality, deemed irredeemable. The state, Foucault says, "takes back with one hand what it seems to exclude with the other. It saves everything" (1979, p. 301).

A crucial part of the work of the *psy-sciences* is to manage both aspiration and its limits in terms of its specialized knowledges and to account for the individual, as object and subject, *to itself* and to others, through making demarcations and breaks. Benjamin, 2006 (pp. 31–32) indicates, the technologies and knowledges of classification and exclusion developed in relation to the technologies of performance and the economy of schooling developed in relation to state schooling.

> The provision of apparently universal schooling drew another kind of attention to the existence of groups of children supposedly

unable to benefit from it. Until the 1870s, one category of mental deficiency—idiocy—had sufficed. The advent of mass, and then compulsory schooling brought with it the perceived need for finer categorisations. A means for excluding the least able working-class children (whose failure to make progress would both inhibit the smooth operation of the school and hold down the payment-by-results salaries of their teachers) was needed. This was found in the introduction of mechanisms for separating children into those who were, and those who were not, deemed able to benefit from instruction. Additional terms had to come into common usage, to account for the children who, whilst they could be deemed unable to profit from elementary schooling, could not be considered as idiots. The terms "imbecile" and "feeble-minded" were already being used interchangeably with idiot (Pritchard, 1963). Their function and meaning began to change in the late 1870s, when arguments for inventing ways of categorising people gained ground. In 1886, the Idiots Act provided for the care and control of idiots *and* imbeciles. This both marked the difference that had been established between the two groups, and made it necessary to develop increasingly sophisticated ways and means of differentiating between them.

Within these relations, in these spaces of definition, particular forms of knowledge are enabled to emerge and provide a conceptual infrastructure for professional practice and a set of operationalized discourses, realized in the "petty, malicious minutiae" (Foucault, 1979, p. 226) of practice. That is to say, "The social sciences have developed in a matrix of power" (Dreyfus & Rabinow, 1983, p. 160). Social policies are both the representation and enactment of management of the population and the opening up of new domains to scientific investigation, based upon a simple reversal in which power seeks invisibility while it makes its objects visible. I want to focus on the work of the norm and the "normalising society" and the psy-sciences at little more, to explore further what Foucault calls "new racism".

Measurement and Residualization and Hereditary Science

The combination of eugenics and statistics made "possible the measurement of overall phenomena, the description of groups, the characterization of collective facts, the calculation of gaps between individuals, their distribution in a given population" (Foucault, 1979, p. 190). They brought into being the modern individual and the normal individual as historical achievements—as "the effect and object of a certain crossing of power and knowledge" (Dreyfus & Rabinow, 1983, p. 160) and this is the major problematic for an effective history of education policy. In this space "both the development of the possibilities of the human and social sciences, and the simultaneous possibility of protecting life and of the holocaust made their historical appearance" (cited in Dreyfus & Rabinow, 1983, p. 138). "Hysterical" and promiscuous young women could be sterilized (see Shoen, 2005) and impaired babies left to die. In Australia, the Queensland Mental Hygiene Act 1938 and the Backward Persons Act 1937 were passed after debate in Parliament which included "Arthur Moore, a member and former leader of the Country Party, describe 'backward' persons as 'a menace to the community, particularly in the propagation of their species' and argued that the only solution 'in the interests of the community and in the interests of these mentally affected people' was sterilization ..." (http://www.probonoaustralia.com.au/news/2012/04/sterilisation-women-disabilities-wa-draft-bill-"appalling").

As noted earlier, in education specifically it was intelligence and its measurement that provided a concept and a set of tools which would professionalize the practice of the teacher and provide a rationale for practice—the division into classes, groups, and streams, the differentiated selection of materials, pacing of coverage, and access to knowledge. Intelligence testing both defined an appropriate education and a set of limits, a fixity—the work of the teacher would be to match an appropriate pedagogy, body of knowledge and pace of coverage to the "needs" and capabilities of individuals, or rather in practice, groups of students who were transmuted from individuals differences (sequences) to distinct types (sets). At each end of this distribution "exceptions" could be located—each in their way abnormal and unteachable, the genius at one end and the backward or "retarded" at the other. Each of whom are "discovered" by testing—education psychology's particular "genre of objectivity" (Burt, 1937). Testing, and the labelling of learners both represented and obscured individuality. The learner is rendered into a category and set of attributes. "Things themselves become so burdened with attributes, signs, allusions that they finally lose their own form. Meaning is no longer read in an immediate perception, the figure no longer speaks for itself" (Foucault, 2001b, p. 16). This overburdened representation creates a space and a language within which the psy-sciences work, and experts talk. Testing and "the examination enabled the teacher, while transmitting his knowledge, to transform his pupils into a whole field of knowledge" (Foucault, 1979, p. 186). The intelligence test took the norm to its "logical" conclusion, that is, as Stobart (2008, p. 30) puts it, "the capacity of assessment to create, rather than to just measure". Individuals were made calculable and subject to the "power of the single number" (Rose, 1999, p. 214). The intelligence test is a form of "statistical anthropology", it asserted an inference, that it could explain what it described, that "your behaviour is intelligent because you are intelligent" (Stobart, 2008, p. 34), and that behaviour and performance have a biological and indeed a genetic "cause", and thus intelligence was inherited, and unevenly distributed, and that measured intelligence was also related to social behaviour and moral reasoning. The circle was squared both in practice and ethics by arguments which linked "fixed" and singular measured intelligences to the distribution of educational opportunities, to the explanation of patterns of antisocial behaviours, to moral worth and thus to the management of the breeding of those social groups of low intellect[8]. Here again the economies of management can be glimpsed and the "external limit of the abnormal" (Foucault, 1979, p. 183) is being sketched, as a scientific, moral and economic frontier, and as a limit to entitlement.

> It is surely unwise to give instruction to students in disregard of their capacities to profit from it, if by enough ingenuity and experimentation we can secure tests which measures their capacities beforehand.
>
> (Thorndike, 1922, p. 7)

> All feeble-minded are at least potential criminals. That every feeble-minded woman is a potential prostitute would hardly be disputed by anyone. Moral judgment, social judgment or any other kind of higher thought process, is a function of intelligence.
>
> (Terman, 1916, p. 11)

> This general intellectual factor, central and all pervading, shows a further characteristic, also disclosed by testing and statistics.

It appears to be inherited, or at least inborn. Neither knowledge nor practice, neither interest nor industry, will avail to increase it.

(Burt, 1937, pp. 10–11)

In 1909, William Beveridge proposed that men who could not work should be supported by the state "but with complete and permanent loss of all citizen rights—including not only the franchise but civil freedom and fatherhood".

(Quoted in Sewell [November 2009], "How eugenics poisoned the welfare state", *The Spectator*)

Here we see again the relation between the delimitation and constitution of a field of knowledge in relation to a form of expertise—statistics—that opens up new professions and professional practices—educational psychology and special education—and creates and legitimates new sites of truth. This "making up of people" consists of what Hacking identifies as five interactive elements—classification, people (the subjects of measurement), institutions, knowledge and experts (Hacking, 1995). "It is at this point in the spread of bio-power that social welfare programs became professionalised" (Dreyfus & Rabinow, 1983, p. 141). Intelligence, testing and statistics as a "combinatory" practice asserts the capacity to represent reality in terms of quantifiable and manipulable domains, and thus render reality as a field of government. Individuality is created and recreated as sets and categories which describe and explain "the population" which is then subject to bio-power, a power which takes hold of human life to "foster it" or "disallow". Statistically derived classifications demarcated the valuable and worthwhile, the productive, from *the residual*.

Those beyond "the external frontier of the abnormal" (Foucault, 1979, p. 183) were deemed as "beyond" schooling, as beyond "reason", even as beyond humanity—as "backward", "feeble-minded" or "crippled", and "confined" in enclosed "total" institutions which were "established on the edges of society" and "turned inwards towards negative functions: arresting evil, breaking communications, suspending time" (p. 209)—all of which are evident in Ernest's entanglement within relations of power.

> We had to go to Sunday school every week and we'd file in crocodiles with a line of boys next to a line of girls. One Sunday one of the girls shouted out, "Ernest Williams touched my knickers". I'd bumped into her accidently as I was walking but I hadn't done anything to her. That was it. I was reported and there was an unholy row. The next morning I was reprimanded in front of the whole school in the hall. I remember I was called out to the front and the headmistress said, "You're worse than the beasts in the field, isn't it boy?'. I was angry because I hadn't done anything and I wouldn't admit to it. I suppose I would have been wiser to have cried and given in. But I remember the authorities couldn't decide what was the best punishment was for my wickedness. They were going to thrash me. Eventually I remember a man saying, "Put him away until he cleanses himself". I was locked in the sick room in solitary confinement with a bread and water diet.
>
> (1926, 11-year-old Ernest Williams, inmate of
> St Helen's Institution for the Blind, Swansea, quoted in
> Humphries & Gordon, 1992, p. 99).

In his "ground breaking" and massively influential book *The Backward Child* (1937) Cyril Burt began with the term "merely backward", but went on to distinguish "this" as sub-normality and separate "dull" from "mentally defective", he claimed to be able to identify the "retarded", the "difficult pupil" and "intellectual abnormalities" (all from 1937)—Oksala's reference to a "zoology of sub-species" (2007, p. 50) again comes to mind. Burt went on to articulate an ethical position, which said that: "each child, therefore, must be considered as a unique individual. His psychological classification is nothing but a means to an end, a practical aid rather than an indisputable point of scientific diagnosis" (p. 14). The "end" is management and discipline. Here again, we can see, in a very detailed sense, what Foucault referred to as "the basic phenomena of the nineteenth century ... what might be called power's hold over life ... that the biological came under state control" (2004a, p. 239).

The psychology of limits, either hereditary or developmental, and their "divigations" in the mundane practices of schools and classrooms, in relation to standards, remains as a practical and discursive recurrence within education policy. "The art of governing required a kind of 'governmentality' related to the role of the state as a definer, watcher, and manager of difference. Hence, the construction of groups and group differences gave rise to identities that were crystallised in many techniques of government by the turn of the twentieth century" (Baker, 1998, p. 132). The psy-sciences as a discursive formation produced and continue to produce new categories and systems of classification which are then inscribed into the everyday practices of institutional life and institutional orderings, in terms of concepts like "intelligence", "ability", "hyperactivity", "normal development", "behavioural difficulties", etc.

Burt (1937) carefully rehearses a variety of "causes" of defectiveness, dullness, etc. and by no means dismisses entirely the role of social conditions and poverty, but these become exactly that, "conditioning" factors rather than causes. After long discussion he concludes "there can be little question that *the chief reasons for educational backwardness are psychological*" (p. 571) and in relation to his case studies he says "in the majority the outstanding cause is a general inferiority of intellectual capacity, presumably inborn and frequently hereditary" (p. 572). Moving to "treatment", he identifies an urgent need for social provision: "the first and foremost step is segregation, the formation of separate classes or schools expressly for the educationally subnormal" (p. 574). Burt goes on to outline a whole infrastructure of professional roles, practices, organizations and architectures for children so identified and the need for further research. Burt's book also offered teachers an amazingly promiscuous and ambiguous vocabulary and "unconsidered modes of thought" which underpin and might be used to identify, divide and describe forms of abnormality. But he also begins to provide for heredity's successor, in outlining the elements of a cultural causation of educational differences, in his discussion for the "intellectual" (p. 126) and "emotional and moral conditions of the home" (p. 129). From this basis, sociologists of education were able to establish an alternative trans-individual account of the "defective child" in which transmission between generations becomes cultural rather than biological, a social heredity of poor parenting, lack of aspiration and a failure to made the home a site of development and pedagogy, a different but not unrelated kind of "fabulation". The family, parenting and childhood are made visible along new dimensions (see Chapter 3).

The duality of education and its limits was firmly established in the late nineteenth and early twentieth hereditarian literature on the "feeble minded". The 1889 Education Department report on *The Education of Defective and Epileptic Children* "had no difficulty in recognising three broad categories—the idiots and imbeciles, the feeble-minded or defective children, and those who could cope with the ordinary curriculum of an elementary school" (Hurt, 1988, p. 129). Maudsley, author the *Psychology and Pathology of the Mind* (1867), asserted that individual differences "are not due to education of circumstances, but a fundamental difference of nature which neither education nor circumstances can eradicate" and as such "great as is the power of education, it is yet a strictly limited power. … No training in the world will avail to elicit grapes from thorns of figs from thistles". Despite the expansion of school medical services and special schools as a form of universal provision from 1913, although with dramatic local variations, it was clear that such services were always most vulnerable in times of financial difficulty. In 1922 Sir George Newman, public health physician, Quaker, first chief medical officer to the Ministry of Health in England, wrote a minute saying that "The Board of Education ought to endeavour to reduce expenditure" on special education "such a reduction being confined as far as possible to the attempted education of defective children whom no education will make breadwinners"—why waste scarce resources on the unproductive.

From the late nineteenth century through to Second World War, the hereditarian analysis, or "fabulation" as Foucault would call it, was rampant. The degenerate "metabody"—the family (see Chapter 3)—and the need of "social defense" against this, was written and rewritten into Reports, Acts and research studies for the whole period, as was the move from a biological to a moral account of the "abnormal individual". Maudsley (1867) wrote of "a destiny made for man by his ancestors, and no one can elude, were he able to attempt it, the tyranny of his organisation". In the work of the Radnor Report (1908), "twenty five of the thirty five witnesses who gave substantial evidence on the issue attached 'supreme importance to the fact that in a very large proportion of cases there is a history of mental defect in the parents or near ancestors'" (Hurt, 1988, p. 137). The Report concluded that "especially in view of the evidence concerning fertility, the prevention of mentally defective persons from becoming parents would tend largely to diminish the numbers of such persons in the population". Indeed, the reverses of the British Army in the Boer War engendered a moral panic concerning the state of the nation's human capital and Hurt (1988, p. 136) comments that the feeble-minded child was seen as posing "a double threat. From him or her there might stem both a physically and a morally degenerate stock". Foucault talks about this sort of reasoning as a "remoralisation at the level of this fantastical etiology" (2003, p. 315).

Social statistics, the science of intelligence, Darwinism and eugenics, in the "tragic and crazy literature" (Foucault, 2003, p. 318) of researchers like Terman, Thorndike, Spearman, Burt, and latterly Eysenk, Jenson, and Hernstein and Murray, are tightly tied together. They underpinned the formation of educational psychology in England, France, Australia and the USA and the establishment of the *British Journal of Educational Psychology*. To return to the point at which we began, the dualities of totalization, division and exclusion articulated by this literature became embedded in basic pedagogical practices and orderings—the lists, sets, "tables", streams and bands, etc.—of schooling, and in the separation of "special" from regular schooling, the demarcation of "impossible learners". These "breaks", both in their institutional and their minute and mundane forms, are enactments of the "breaks" in the species identified by Foucault, *they are rooted in blood—both measured and spilled*. They are also the precise, humane and operational bases for government, for discipline and regulation, a form of power vested in scientific truths and measurements, in pedagogies and pastoral care. *Here, rather than the "humanity" of the learner as the legal limit of educational practices, education is used to define the legal limit to humanity.*

3

A THOROUGHLY MODERN EDUCATION—BLOOD FLOWS THROUGH IT!

Foucault's work seeks to uncover not the development of rationality, but the ways news forms of control and power are legitimated by complex discourses that stake a claim to rationality and that are embedded in diverse institutional sites.

(Olssen, 1993, p. 2)

In this chapter I will pursue further the lines of genealogical enquiry begun in the previous chapter, bringing them more up to date and tracing both shifts and continuities in the relations of blood and racism, again employing Foucault's meaning of the term, to regulation and discipline, within education policy. This will also involve exploring a little further the play of technologies which cover the "surface" that lies between discipline and regulation, "between the organic and the biological, between body and population" (Foucault, 2004a, p. 253). That is, I will indicate some ways in which "breaks" and classifications, and concomitant exclusions, are applied to the body and population within policy and within classrooms, pausing at four educational moments in the present to explore these: (1) Primary schooling in relation to the National Strategies and National Testing; (2) School standards in relation to institutional and international competitiveness; (3) Race in relation to "new IQism", exclusion, the cultural pathology of families, and nature and danger; (4) Special Educational Needs in relation to the politics of inclusion and exclusion. I will conclude with some general comments about exclusion in contemporary schooling drawing on the work of Nikolas Rose and Mitchell Dean.

I want to indicate the history of and relations among some of the technologies, problematizations, classifications and exclusions and some of the "unconsidered modes of thought [on which] the practices that we accept rest ..." (Foucault, 1988b, p. 154), which were sketched in the previous chapter, as they come into view in the present, and come together to construct education policy and practice. The point about *coming together* is important—Armstrong (2009, p. 441) quotes Foucault in contrasting the "simple configurations" of events with essential traits and final meanings, with what is "on the contrary ... a profusion of entangled events", which are, in turn, as Prado (1995, p. 38) says, the "products of conglomerations of blind forces". The chapter will explore some of these entanglements and blindness.

Hidden Voices: The Exile and The Leper

On 1 April, local education authorities became responsible for the education of severely handicapped children hitherto considered to be "unsuitable for education at school". Now for the first time in history all children without exception are within the scope of the educational system. The Education (Handicapped Children) Act of 1970 is the last milestone—along the road starting with the Education Act of 1870, which set out to establish a national system of education.

(Margaret Thatcher, Bristol, April 1970,
www.margaretthatcher.org/document/102105)

This Act can be viewed as the end of exclusion, of one sort, or perhaps a reworking of the boundaries of normality. An English national system of education was created not in 1870 but in 1970. Why do we not attend to this?

Given this, what does education policy research look like if, like Foucault, we start from the outside, from the point of view of obscure and obscured individuals who cannot, by categorization speak for themselves, who are "special" or "abnormal", those who do not fit, and who are deemed "unfit"? What happens if we think about their encounters with power and turn our attention to their hidden history? A history that is, in part at least, *Out of Sight* (Humphries & Gordon, 1992)—a history of abnormality and a history of blood, a subjugated and subjugating history, on the outside of education, literally and analytically—a history of exclusion, and its "resilience" and "ubiquity" (Slee, 2011, p. 150); a history of the manufacture of abnormal subjects, and their proliferation—marked and demarcated by "typological obsession" (Armstrong, 2009, p. 442).

Many people have already contributed to such a history— Armstrong, Allan, Barton, Hurt, Slee, Tomlinson, the writers of Critical Race Theory and of post-colonial studies, and many, many others. I am not intending to over-write their work, rather I want to reposition education policy studies in relation to this work. We normally look at special education or inclusive education policy or race and education, if we bother at all, as fields for special specialists, experts of their very own. At best, in "our" work, these specialisms are left as a dangling comma-izations of "other" inequalities and oppressions (Troyna, 1994). These are viewed dimly from the perspective of the mainstream, looking outward to "the other". Special education is formed and formulated in relation to normal education or as Slee (2011) points out, what we call "regular schooling". Those subject to such "special" attention are defined within academic practice and research by their irregularity and their relative invisibility from the "mainstream", with their own courses, associations, journals, and tucked away in the additional clauses or end pieces of Acts and White Papers, discussed on specialist websites rather than the "popular" media, and hidden in the "back regions" of schools as "outcasts on the inside" (Bourdieu & Champagne, 1999, p. 422), or exiled in Pupil Referral Units, as afterthoughts, footnotes and special cases. As Graham and Slee (2008) say "to include is not necessarily to be inclusive". The irregular are not part of education policy, but nonetheless define, underpin, and specify it.

We might do education policy studies differently by exploring the tightly related and overlapping genealogies of classifications and of blood, or what Foucault calls "the model of exclusion" and its concomitants "disqualification, exile, rejection, deprivation, refusal and incomprehension … an entire arsenal of negative concepts" (2003, pp. 43–44). These arise despite and in part because of their articulation with "positive" techniques of "intervention and transformation". The proliferation of knowledges of the abnormal and their "psychologico-moral point of view" (p. 295) is "a certain form of exercise of power" (p. 219) that remains fundamental to understanding contemporary educational "abnormalities".

Foucault said that "critique is not a matter of saying that things are not right as they are. It is a matter of pointing out on what kinds of assumptions, what kinds of familiar, unchallenged and unconsidered modes of thought the practices that we accept rest" (1988b, pp. 154–155). This is what I am trying to do by tracing the emergence and fusion of an inter-related set of educational "fabulations" across the nineteenth and twentieth centuries and into the twenty-first. The work these "fabulations" and their conflation are not confined to the leper and the exile and the "dangerous" and the "defective", rather the fields of race and special education provide a set of concepts and practices and classifications which are generalized across pedagogy as a whole. The enactments of classification and division, the "inclusion paradox" as Slee (2011) calls it, is fundamental to the practice of pedagogy (discipline) and the management of the school population (regulation).

> Historically, formal educational structures in England are grounded in systems, structures, processes and curricula based on the division, assessment and categorisation of learners. These divisions have taken place according to formal and informal measures relating to place, class, gender, race, perceived ability and disability, academic performance and assumptions about learners.
>
> (Armstrong, 2009, p. 443)

History in the Present

In the previous chapter I sought to sketch some of the limits of modern education policy discourse and to render the history of education policy as a set of fictions. This is a move towards what White (1978, p. 233) calls the "disremembrance of things past". Does this enable us to ask "what is our present?" Can we call into question, call to account, the modes of thought that we deploy or which perhaps more appropriately deploy us, in the making and remaking of education through policy? Foucault asserts that our own times and lives are not the beginning or end of some "historical" process, but a period like, while at the same time unlike, any other. I want to point to an absence of "turning points", of "progress" and discontinuities and the non-emergence of new forms of reasoning and highlight instead the continuities of the specifics of *division*. In *Discipline and Punish*, Foucault sees the particular point at which the limits of present are apparent as "The constant division between the normal and the abnormal, to which every individual is subjected". That is:

> ... by applying the binary branding and exile of the leper to quite different objects; the existence of a whole set of techniques and institutions for measuring, supervising and correcting the abnormal brings into play the disciplinary mechanisms to which the fear of the plague gave rise. All the mechanisms of power which, even today, are disposed around the abnormal individual, to brand him and to alter him, are composed of those two forms from which they distantly derive—the exile and the leper.
>
> (1979, p. 198)

This is the present I set out to explore here—that of the exile and the leper, that of race and social class and disability. To be clear, this is not the story of how "the seamless web of yester-year" leads slowly and inexorably into the present. Rather I am trying to underline our embeddedness within the modes of reasoning of "the modern". The past I described in the previous chapter is not alien and irrational, it is who we are in the present, and it is modernity in its past and present forms. As Dreyfus and Rabinow explain, sometimes: "genealogy … finds recurrences and play where others found progress and seriousness" (1983, p. 106). Progress needs to be disturbed. Genealogical knowledge, Foucault said, was for "cutting" and "dissociating", not understanding (1991a, p. 90). It is based in the value of "refusal", the use of imagination and the deploy-ment of irony. As Roth (1981) puts it, "Foucault uncovers the past to rupture the present into a future that will leave the very function of history behind it; a future that will have no need of *a past to be endlessly recaptured*, but that will be situated merely 'in the scattering of the profound stream of time'" (p. 44, emphasis added). Or to put it another way, the point is not to make sense of our history in the present but to make it unac-ceptable. It is about questioning the history that enfolds us, as a violent imposition of truth. The genealogist does not "use history to lament the wandering away from a past ideal or the failure to move toward an ideal future, but to point to current dangers" (Shapiro, 1992, p. 11). In some ways, a different future may be better glimpsed from outside progress than within it (see Allan, 2003).

Clearly, again, I cannot do proper justice to these tasks in the space available. What I will try to do is to point to some traces, recurrences, circularities and iterations of the forms of "branding" and "alteration" discussed previously, occurring "in the present", both those that are dramatic and those that are mundane, and attend to the histories of "obscure people" and "local memories", or what Ainscow, Booth et al. (1999) call "hidden voices".

From Tainted Blood, to Pathologies of Culture and the Metabody

> Effective history never forgets or obscures its own temporal and cultural situatedness, as well as the cultural and temporal contexts of its subjects, and it rejects as absurd the idea that history can be done objectively, that it can be done from no particular point of view.
>
> (Prado, 1995, p. 41)

This is where I come in. This is where my autobiography makes itself known. I am a sociologist of education; I am a part of the history I seek to rework, situated within it in complicated ways. As noted earlier in rewriting this history I am also rewriting myself. Foucault said that anytime he tried to carry out a piece of theoretical work, "it has been on the basis of my own experience; always in relation to processes I saw taking place around me. It is because I thought I could recognise in the things I saw, in the institutions with which I dealt, in my relations with others, cracks, silent shocks, malfunctionings ... that I undertook a particular piece of work, *a few fragments of an autobiography*" (cited in Simons, 1995, p. 8). Our own knowledges and practices as sociologists, pedagogues, philosophers, policy analysts, are historically implicated, and continue to be implicated, in the practices of the management of the population, and the construction and maintenance of social and racial divisions. The sociology of education came into existence in the nexus of population and policy.

In 1932, in response to pressure from the Eugenics Society the UK Minister of Health established a government committee (the Brock Committee) to report on the possibility of the enforced sterilization of the "feeble minded" to address the problem of uneven reproduction across the social classes. At this time eugenics was a widely accepted mode of reasoning within Fabianism and at the London School of Economics. Eugenicist views were espoused by "respectable" thinkers, like H. G. Wells, J. M. Keynes, Julian Huxley, and William Beveridge, and the latter three all sat on the Council of the Eugenics Society. As late as 1946, shortly before his death, Keynes declared eugenics to be "the most important, significant and, I would add, genuine branch of sociology which exists" (Keynes, 1946, p. 39). This sits starkly in relation to Foucault's assertion that, as with other projects of perfection, "socialism has made no critique of the theme of biopower" (2004a, p. 261).

However, set over and against the eugenics lobby was among others, Lancelot Hogben "the first, last and only" professor of Social Biology at the LSE (1930–37)[1], whose department undertook mathematical investigations bearing on human genetics, population growth, differential fertility and (with Louis Herrman) the responses of monozygotic and dizygotic twins to intelligence tests. His department became a centre for demography research. Hogben was an outspoken anti-eugenicist and his book *Political Arithmetic* (1938) was published in part as a response to the eugenicist panic in the 1930s around the issue of population decline and social class differentials in birth rates and ensuing debates about appropriate policy responses. One of the instigators of the debate was Enid Charles, his wife and a lecturer in his department at

LSE, whose book *The Twilight of Parenthood*; when re-published in 1936, bore the title *The Menace of Under-Population* (Charles, 1936). There were two distinct positions in this debate: the eugenicists were concerned that the "wrong" citizens were reproducing while the "right" ones were not, leading to calls for forced sterilization; whereas those like Hogben, argued for better use to be made of the population through raising the school leaving age and by introducing universal secondary education, anticipating the post-war "waste of talent" discourse. Both positions sit firmly within the problematics of the population as a *resource to be managed*. As Eggleston (1976, p. 127) noted: "The social distribution of education identified by the research of sociologists became re-identified as the social maldistribution of educational opportunity" and "Their evidence was used to particularly powerful effect by the advocates of secondary school reorganisation."

Two different versions of population management as a political and scientific problem in relation to the "well-being of the state" were in contest here—one regulatory and one disciplinary. On one side were those who believed in the necessity of the exercise of biopower in regulation of the "blood" of the nation and reproductive practices, seeing the use of state power as essential to its "life". Ranged against them were those who trusted to the more subtle disciplines of social welfare aimed at the behaviour of individuals in the social body. These are different points of emphasis in the "triangle, sovereignty-discipline-government, which has the population as its primary target" (Foucault, 1996). The eugenicists represented and argued for a form of sovereign/regulatory power which would be enacted directly upon the bodies of those parts of the population deemed to be responsible for the reproduction of dangerous and debilitating traits and behaviours. In contrast the "sociologists" were articulating a form of disciplinary/governmental power to be exercised through the institutions of education and the professional knowledge and practices of teachers, and welfare interventions into the lives of "poor" families.

In 1934 the Brock Committee recommended in favor of a programme of "voluntary sterilisation". A recommendation that was in fact "quietly forgotten as the cruelty of compulsory sterilisation in Nazi Germany was exposed from the mid-1930s" (King & Hansen, 1999, p. 83). However, as noted in Chapter 2, sterilization programmes did become law in Sweden, Australia, parts of the US, and other countries (see Spektorowski & Mizrachi, 2004).

It was the interventionist/welfarist/disciplinary approach rather than eugenics, which dominated the post-war social reconstruction of Britain and placed education as one of the pillars of a modern welfare state. *However, the modes of thought on which this reconstruction drew are not significantly different from eugenics and that in many ways eugenic modes of thought remain thoroughly ingrained within education policy and practice.* That is to say, alongside the residues of genetic accounts of normality and difference, forms of culture, life style and relationships within the family, were identified by sociologists as a new grid of intelligibility within which educational success and failure could be located. The family became a new space of social rationality, and pathology. The *socialising family* became an object of research, and latterly of increasing control and intervention, organized around a new problematic and object of knowledge that we call *parenting* (see Vincent, 2012). A new iteration of *degeneracy* comes into view in relation to the pathological family, the abnormal family (see below), set in direct contrast to what Musgrove (1970) quite simply called "the good home". There emerged two key elements to this pathology, one a failure of discipline and the other a failure of aspiration. The failures of the family are "passed on" as a form of social heredity, as outlined by Burt (1937), in "cycles of disadvantage" (Chapter 2). Tellingly, Jean Floud, one the first generation of post-war British sociologists, borrowed the term "*la famille educogene*" to refer to homes that foster an educative climate, and the family whose attitudes and orientations are congruent with the demands and the aims of the school. Here, blood is rearticulated as culture, as another version of hereditarianism. There is new interplay of measurement and morality, elicited in attitudinal surveys or N-Ach scores, as these were statistically related to patterns of school access and performance. A new form of sociological norm was articulated over and against but also alongside the psychological. Maurice Craft outlined the lines of the grid:

> The influence of "home background" upon school achievement is a familiar theme in educational research, government reports, and journalistic comment. This collection of readings seeks to give greater precision to what is meant by home background, and shed some light on its very complex relationships with a child's school performance.
>
> (Editor's preface, Craft, 1970)

Within this new field, in different ways, the "metabody", the "huge fantastical body of the family" (Foucault, 2006b, pp. 270–271) is causal. This is played out in relation to the new form of family relationships which emerged in the nineteenth century based on "the solidification and intensification of father–mother–children relationships" (2003, p. 327) and a reversal of family obligations, of parents for children. "The family became an instrument, a point of application, in the monitoring of a larger group (the population), rather than a unit concerned with monitoring itself" (Baker, 1998, p. 131). In this way social problems, like migration, housing, crime, literacy, and social disorder (see below)—are transformed into biological problems, problems of blood and "race". The state took responsibility for the management of these problems through its newly created institutions and programmes, and through the work of state professions and the application of new "knowledges" and "sciences" of the social. This social hereditarianism and the needs of population management have again become very clear in the responses to the 2011 riots in England.

> Wed, 10 Aug 2011
>
> The Prime Minister, David Cameron, has hit out at the rioters for "a complete lack of responsibility, a lack of proper parenting, a lack of proper upbringing, a lack of proper ethics, a lack of proper morals".
>
> I can announce today that over the next few weeks, I and ministers from across the Coalition government will review every aspect of our work to mend our broken society, on schools, welfare, families, parenting, addiction, communities, on the cultural, legal, bureaucratic problems in our society too ...
>
> This not about poverty, it's about culture—a culture that glorifies crime. In too many cases, the parents of these children—if they are still around—don't care where their children are or who they are with; let alone what they are doing.

Indeed, the relations of sociology to policy and the hereditarian thematic, and continuities with the nineteenth century, also came into view in the 1970s (and again in the 1990s) in relation to the concept of "cycles of deprivation", which in the 1970s attracted interest and support from Conservative neo-liberal politician and writer Keith Joseph.

> In particular, Joseph's interest in low-income families was of a particular kind, and closely bound up with the concept of the problem family. This essentially behavioral explanation of poverty and deprivation, that emphasised household squalor and inadequate parenting, exercised an important influence over public health doctors, social workers, and voluntary organisations in the 1940–70 period. In 1966, for example, Joseph had included among categories of need, problem families whose poverty was not caused primarily by lack of income, but by difficulties in managing money and in using welfare services. Along with the better-known Edgbaston speech (October 1974), Joseph's cycle hypothesis illustrates marked continuities between late-nineteenth and late-twentieth century thought on poverty, placing it squarely within the longer-term history of recurring underclass stereotypes over the past 120 years.
>
> (Welshman, n.d., p. 5)

> ESRC decided to hold this conference to help broaden Treasury links with sociologists and social policy specialists. The theme was a revisiting in the light of new evidence of the idea of "cycles of deprivation" which was the subject of a major initiative (on transmitted deprivation) by the then SSRC and DHSS in the 1970s, following a major speech on the subject by Sir Keith Joseph. He was intrigued by the contrast between an increase in living standards co-existing with the existence of a group of people who were in poverty and underachieving and re-creating itself.
>
> (Lee and Hills, 1998, p. iii)

Post-World War II sociology established a different mode of thought for education policy, but one which was not as different as all that, one which overlaid the direct relation of blood to policy and to regulation, with a set of more indirect relationships mediated by culture and by parenting—by the "metabody"—to discipline.

A similar, but partial displacement of blood from genes to culture is evident in relation to contemporary forms of what Foucault calls "ethnic racism". Barker noted in his book *The New Racism* (1981), how traditional biological and genetic formulations of racist belief seemed to be ebbing away and were being replaced by culturalist ones, defining subordinate "racial" groups as inferior because of their way of life and therefore inappropriate to the nation to which they had been forced or emigrated or fled as refugees, rather than their skin colour.

Nonetheless, throughout all of this, via its tropes of intelligence and intelligence testing, eugenics had in a whole variety of ways "done is work" and ensconced itself firmly within policy, in institutional and classroom practices, and in the language and concepts of teaching. The bi- and tri-partite systems of secondary education set in place by the 1944 Education Act in England were based upon principles of ability measurement, which included intelligence testing. The Norwood Report (1943) which recommended the tri-partite system, drew on eugenicist thinking, and established "breaks" which were then translated into policy, in its confident assertion that the education system had "thrown up" three "rough groupings" of children with three different "types of mind". These esconcements are clearly pointed out by Chitty (2009), Gillborn and Youdell (2000), Lowe (1998) and White (2006);

all four argue that eugenics continues to be a foundational mode of thought for contemporary education. Lowe (1998) sees a clear eugenicist strand in the contemporary obsession with testing used to identify different "ability levels" matched to "appropriate" learning experiences; Gillborn and Youdell (2000, p. 212) maintain that: "The view of 'ability' that currently dominates education, from the heart of government through to individual classrooms, represents a victory for the hereditarian position"; and White (2006, p. 141) argues that the current interest in multiple intelligences has "central features in common" with "the traditional view about the nature of intelligence", specifically, "in its belief in the innate basis of the intelligences and in its intellectualist orientation". This mode thought is also evident in relation to race and gender and education policy.

> Issues of differential intelligence among racial and gendered groups in society seem still to capture the popular imagination even now, 150 years since the rise of social Darwinism. Press reports of black people as less intelligent have been aroused recently in the UK by the publication of *The Bell Curve* in the USA. Similarly, reports that girls may be outperforming boys in examination results have invoked much media attention, reviving issues of differential genetic capacities between the sexes. At the end of the twentieth century ideas about innate, genetic, scientifically provable difference are still at the heart of our thinking about race and gender.
>
> (Mirza, 1998, p. 109)

Class, race, disability and blood intertwine within education policy and practice, constantly re-emerging in different forms and contexts and guises, always in relation to power. They intersect very directly for example in Bernard Coard's account of *How the West Indian Child is Made Educationally Sub-Normal by the British School System* (1971).

> The Black child acquires two fundamental attitudes of beliefs as a result of his experiencing the British school system: a low self-image, and consequently low self-expectations in life. These are obtained through streaming, banding, bussing ESN schools, racist news media, and a white middle-class curriculum.
>
> (p. 31)

They continue to work to *brand*, divide off and *exile* African-Caribbean boys in particular (see Graham, 2011) and they recur in *The Bell Curve*, and are manifest in the fears produced in response to the construction of black boys as "naturally" dangerous.

> An ensemble of images of black boys as "dangerous thugs" or as an "endangered species" means that black youth violence or educational failure, unlike that of white youth, prompts little soul searching in America. It is expected, seen as "inherent in the kids themselves" as natural (or maybe cultural) expression of black racial difference.
>
> (Tilton, 2000, p. 143)

Ferguson, in her book *Bad Boys: Public Schools and the Making of Black Masculinity* (2000), argues that black children, especially boys are seen as "not child-like" at all, rather in effect as "unnatural".

Within contemporary education, educational research and social policy, and in the practices of schools and aspirations of teachers, morality and "intelligence" have become tightly "entangled" in relation to social class, race and disability. Blood and culture are fused, and the normal family has become increasingly directly tied to the paradigm of the middle class, and to the moral attribute of "deserving". Moral panics around patterns of reproduction, as in the 1930s, are regularly played out around "threats" to society and "enemies within" and the spectre of the breakdown of social and moral order. Differential patterns of achievement are "explained" by deficits of aspiration or lack of parental control, or "natural" inequalities. In these ways, the problem of population, its management and its productivity remain as the main themes of education policy in the twenty-first century, from the "mobilisation of talent in industrial societies" (Floud, 1970, p. 31), to "international competitiveness" and "our economic growth and our country's future" (Department for Education, 2010, p. 3). Techniques, practices which emerged in the nineteenth century and continue to organize, articulate and animate public debate, research and mundane classroom decision-making. There is a double continuity, the work of a new "mode of thought"—sociology—intertwined with the old—eugenics—in an uneasy but "productive" relation, and not all that different in form or function. This continuity is currently being played out in a new iteration of the measurement of performance in relation to the politics of race, social class and education and the politics of inclusion, which I will explore briefly.

Who Are You? Who is it Possible to be?

Policy and research construct objects of knowledge and subjects of intervention. They create possibilities for *who we are and might be,* both in public policy discourse and institutional practices. I will look briefly at four moments, or points, on the "carceral continuum", where policy and practice, regulation and discipline intersect and subjects are produced. These are no more than markers, which need to be returned to.

1. Turning the tables: Primary schooling in relation to the National Strategies and National Testing.

So let us fast-forward to a socially diverse, twenty-first century, urban, Year 1, "elementary" school classroom in London, in an 1886 board school building, that features in Claudine Rausch's doctoral research (2012). The classroom is organized into tables "by ability"—the children on these tables are named as circles, triangles, squares and hexagons. The complexity of the shape somehow represents the complexity of the child, or the child's mind. The teacher explains the classroom thus:

> And I have my, my very bottom group, there's only three children. Then my middle group this year is actually the two next groups. And my top group are the two higher groups. 'Cause it's meant to be quite a high ability class. So the top 12 children all do the higher abil-ity work. Whereas some classes, last year for example my top group was only the six children in the very, very top group, my middle group were the next two down and the lower ability groups were the next two.

Rausch comments that what we see here is "the residue of 'fixed' notions of ability based 'on the psychology of the last century' (Hill, 2005, p. 88) operant in the ways in which children are organized, talked about and taught into the new millennium" (p. 21). Here there is a plethora of finely differentiated gradients, fixed and changing, within the organization of the classroom into a cellular arrangement of "divisible segments" (Foucault, 1979, p. 163) which are populated by students with different "abilities", and "speeds" of acquisition. The classroom and the teacher's work are structured by "breaks" in the biological continuum of ability. Class work is designed for students in relation to these speeds and their essential cognitive characteristics and they are subject to interventions that are designed to "fix and repair" divergence from the norms of pacing of knowledge, in this case set in relation to national "levels" of achievement. These demarcations and interventions are points "where power reaches into the very grain of individuals" (Foucault, 1980a, p. 39). These minute and multitudinous, small "breaks" map onto more general ones, the organization of bodies in the classroom relates to the social structure of the population—working class students are over-represented on the "bottom" tables, while there are no Black-Caribbean children on the "top" table. Within the mundane techniques of what Foucault calls "new racism" the classroom is divided into "types" and these are rank ordered and distributed into hierarchical tables, scales and catalogues (Foucault, 1970b, p. 71). The teacher goes on to explain the relation between the "abilities" of the tables and the setting of appropriate levels of work and Rausch comments:

> It is a small point, but I am slightly intrigued by the phrase "setting three levels of ability work-wise" as to me it hints at this process of children and their "abilities" being *made* in this process. Setting three levels of ability work-wise describes to me this process that starts with the "work" or "objectives" as defined by the National

Strategy documents, then "sets" three levels of ability into which children, with their erstwhile heterogeneity are allocated to homogenous organisational groupings. Thinking about a liquid solidifying, or "setting" provides for me an image of the ways in which children in this schooling context appeared to become set or fixed in and by their allocated "ability" and its co-location.

(p. 25)

We can see in this classroom a "degree of order, a degree discipline, and regularity, reaching inside the body" (Foucault, 2006b, p.4), the operation of the *pedagogical gaze* and "its neutrality, and the possibility of its gaining access to the object, in short, the effective condition of possibility of the relationship of objectivity", the validity of which is founded on "a relationship of order, a distribution of time, space, and individuals" (Foucault, 2006b, p.4). Here an "optics of truth" is linked in very practical and mundane ways to the production of "objectified subjects". The learners are organized for teaching purposes and encouraged to view themselves in terms of the paradigm of ability and its "normal" distribution. This is made very evident in their allocation to tables. Also perhaps here the intersection of archeology and genealogy comes into view again. The classroom becomes a "natural history" of learners, who are laid out Linnaeus-like, on their tables in their biological natural order—visible, classified, each defined by its essential "character" (Foucault, 1970b, p. 139), separated from one another by their hereditary "differences" (p. 142)— "once the system of variables—the character—has been defined at the outset, it is no longer possible to modify it" (p. 143). Character and differences are made visible by a heady combination of *classical* observation and *modernist* testing.

In "ordinary" classrooms like these, pedagogy, as a set of technologies, works "to set up and preserve an increasingly differentiated set of anomalies, which is the very way it extends its knowledge and power into wider and wider domains" (Dreyfus & Rabinow, 1983, p. 198). The application of these knowledges draws upon the use of inventions and individualized programmes, and the work of "therapists" and specialized learning assistants of various kinds to "fix" and "repair" these anomalies (Bernstein 1990). Even so some children remain beyond "normal" possibilities of repair, they are re-defined as pastoral or legal or medical subjects, and internally or externally exiled (Rausch, 2012).

2. School standards in relation to institutional processes and international competitiveness:

Let us look, again briefly, at another twenty-first century classroom setting and another piece of research. In this case, the classrooms of four "ordinary" secondary schools (see Ball et al., 2012) set harshly within the "gaze of policy", in ways not unlike the nineteenth century. That is, subject to an overbearing "focus" on raising standards, set within a framework of market relations between schools, and performance-related funding. Both New Labour and the current UK Coalition government set great store by school performance as a measure of the health of the education system, tightly tied to the needs of international economic competitiveness. Schools are made responsible for the "population-wealth problem" (Foucault, 2009, p. 365). Indeed schools are overburdened with responsibilities for the population "as a general system of living beings" (p. 366)—its reproduction and sexuality (Ringrose, 2011), its size and shape (Evans, Rich et al., 2008), its health and well-being. Schools are now more than ever vehicles for government reason and regulation. They are thoroughly implicated within a "political economy" of education and have been made responsive to the signals and requirements of performance represented in League Tables—yet another sort of "natural history" and of visibility and ranking—and performance indicators, further set in relation to parental choice and benchmarks set by government. This is *dispositif* of education reform.

> So much of the education debate in this country is backward looking: have standards fallen? Have exams got easier? These debates will continue, but what really matters is how we're doing compared with our international competitors. That is what will define our economic growth and our country's future. The truth is, at the moment we are standing still while others race past. In the most recent OECD PISA survey in 2006 we fell from 4th in the world in the 2000 survey to 14th in science, 7th to 17th in literacy, and 8th to 24th in mathematics.
>
> (Preface to Department for Education, 2010)

The past is eschewed in this extract, but the future is, in terms of the analysis developed here, defined by it; "a past to be endlessly recaptured" (Shapiro, 1992, p. 11). The nation, its schools, teachers and individual students (as in the examples above and below) are captured in a matrix of calculabilities. Within what (Ozga, 2008) calls "governing knowledge"; that is, a regime of numbers—a "resource through which surveillance can be exercised" (p. 264)—addressed to improvements in quality and efficiency, by making nations, schools and students "legible" (p. 268). Optics, objectivities and productivity are tightly intertwined here in a general method of government, which was developed and generalized in the nineteenth century. These "numbers" are deployed within schemes like the Programme for International Student Assessment (PISA)—from which, tellingly, students with "special needs" are excluded—national evaluation systems, school performance tables, test comparisons, throughput and equity indicators, etc. (Rinne, Kallo et al., 2004). These measures are increasingly important in the ways that states monitor, steer and reform their education systems at every level and in every sector. That is, "the technology of statistics creates the capacity to relate to reality as a field of government" (Hunter, 1996, p. 154). Or as Rose indicates:

> In analyses of democracy, a focus on numbers is instructive, for it helps us turn our eyes from the grand texts of philosophy to the mundane practices of pedagogy, of counting, of information and polling, and to the mundane knowledges of "grey sciences" that support them.
>
> (1999, p. 232)

For teachers the pressures of the regime of numbers defines "a whole field of new realities" (Foucault, 2009, p. 75) and the "pertinent space within which and regarding which" (p. 75) they must act. Schooling as a process is rendered into an input–output calculation. Teachers work extraordinarily hard to monitor and improve student performances, nonetheless, more than ever before, one effect of this is that the population of students is effectively "divided up, distributed and fixed" (p. 69). This is done by the application of changing categories and terms which "implies an always finer approximation of power to individuals" (p. 46). Schools can now buy specially designed software that will enable "focus", comparison and identification, as for example, the aptly named *Pupil Asset*

(See Figure 3.1) that enables the "tracking" of student performance, the mapping of "actuals" in relation to "targets", the calculation of "point scores" and "value-added"—quickly, clearly and simply.

Here the student population is assessed and "valued", and invested in, as a resource for the school and indirectly the nation. Again though this is also a moral economy, an economy of student worth, of value *and* values.

... so this is our assessment that you're just seeing there. So when they come, they come with Key Stage 2, which I've converted into a two decimal place by interpolation. Their year 7 target will be 14% on that ... from the line of best fit, it looked like a 14% increase was a

Figure 3.1 Pupil Asset Software.

decent sort of figure to work with ... its quite fine lines if you're doing percentages, it's not As Bs and Cs.

(Martin, George Elliott School, Maths)

... there's been a lot closer monitoring of how students are progressing, there's much more emphasis on analyzing the data, any student who isn't making their three levels of progress over two Key Stages would be a focus for intervention.

(Nicola, Atwood School, English)

The word "focus" was used repeatedly in interviews in this research (Ball, Maguire et al., 2011) to describe the orientation of schools and staff to the question of standards at all levels. One assistant head at Atwood School (Caroline) uses the word 32 times in her interview almost always in reference to standard raising—as in:

... keeping a really strong focus on you should be, you know, increasing two levels over three years, so two-thirds of a level this year and then reporting that to parents.

... making teachers traffic lighting the data so that the teachers are aware of the students that they need to focus on... (see "triage" below)

So there's all stuff like that, which is really, really good and it would just be much better to just focus, say, "Okay, we're going to keep the focus up on Assessment for Learning. Assessment for Learning is really important."

The word "focus" is interesting. It suggests the idea of bringing a lens to bear, a close-up view, a point of concentration, bringing things into visibility. It also suggests precise, organized and efficient action. It is also used in relation to different subjects and objects. That is, teachers, students and schools, and pedagogies, procedures, performance, data and initiatives, all of these objects and subjects are to be "focused" *on*, in order to raise standards (Perryman, Ball et al., 2011). "The student, teacher and school are each subject to the gaze of the next, and all are subject to the gaze of the state" (Youdell, 2011, p. 37). As Foucault (1979, p. 187) explains disciplinary power—"imposes on those whom it subjects a principle of compulsory visibility … it is the fact of being constantly seen, of being always able to be seen, that maintains the disciplined subject in his subjections". The primary and ultimate point of focus is on students as productive subjects, as "abilities-machines" (Foucault, 2010b, p. 229) or, as we shall see, more precisely the focus is on some students in particular. One effect of their visibility is also their classification, that is, "the objectification of those who are subjected" (Foucault, 1979) but within all of this teachers are also brought into the gaze of judgment.

[T]he deputy heads of year have been given a responsibility that they look at the data and they focus on which are the groups of students that we need to focus on, so that's, that's been built into the culture of the school.

(Caroline, Atwood, SLT)

I'm slightly dreading the summer because this is my first results summer as head of department so I can't tell you exactly how this will be. I know the heads of core subjects [English and Maths] have interviews with the head pretty much immediately at the beginning of term, which go on for a number of hours, where you go through all of the results and you will be asked a lot of questions … that's quite nerve wracking.

(Nicola, Atwood, English)

Students are objectified as talented, borderline, underachieving, irredeemable, etc. and as external policy decisions change the metrics of performance, this is refracted in changes of emphasis within the schools to "focus" on and produce different sorts of students.

> We're not allowed to focus on that any more [value added] which was really demoralising because maybe we're going to be picking out different kids now … there was C/D borderline intervention last year, more so than was done in the past and it looks like it is going to be stepped-up.
>
> (Naomi, Atwood, RE)

There is a marked paradox here in that the techniques of policy which rest upon the granting of greater autonomy to institutions and processes of deconcentration within education systems, set within a model of marketization and competition, provide the state with new modes of governing society and the economy, and the shaping and reshaping of individuals and individual conduct—teachers and learners. Here the scope and meaning of government, which has the economy as its principal object, is extended into the minutiae of classroom processes and teacher–student interactions, as a new "level of reality and a field of intervention for government" (Foucault, 2009, p. 97). The teacher is "nudged" or perhaps in this case "shoved" by the techniques of economic behaviourism (Thaler & Sunstein, 2008) into the practices of strategic economic rationality. This involves a reworking of the state itself, and its relation to the population and the school. The teacher and the student are made into "enterprises" (Foucault, 2010b, p. 173) within a "renewed capitalism", in relation to which the state is the regulator and market-maker. However, I digress and I will return to these changing forms of governmentality in the next chapter. The point I want to make here is that the logic of performance and productivity once again produces the effect of residualization, the "breaks" established between those who are worth "investing" in and those who are not—new "lepers"—is the process that Gillborn and Youdell (2000) call *triage*. This is a form of moral and economic decision-making, the assignment of value and a redesignation of values. In local economies of student worth, where they are able, schools act strategically to avoid these lepers, costly and unproductive students—those with special needs, behavioural difficulties, unsupportive parents, or another mother tongue. Again limits are set to the extension of schooling, the lepers, shunned and feared are exiled, their behaviour or "character" is seen as detrimental to learning, others are subject to forms of "enclosure"— they are seen as threats to performance and the raising of standards.

The last two moments of pause are again very brief and very superficial, and it is important to say that there is nothing new here, except the viewpoint and the attempt to see things together, as dispersion and as an organization. At each moment there is a particular combination of division, fixing, and exclusion—a setting of boundaries—a relation of productivity to resources, and a morality. Again these are set within a grid of intelligibility in which blood and its surrogates—intelligence, ability, culture, race and gender— naturalize (literally) and legitimate, complex and changing systems of management, calculation and care[2].

3. New IQism and "new" and "old" racism

The redeployment of intelligence, as ability, in relation again to "breaks in the species" and mundane classifications, was already noted in Rausch's work and Coard's study.

Gillborn (2010a) says: "As with the classic IQism of the nine-teenth and twentieth centuries, contemporary policy in the UK typically envisages a tripartite division in human abilities: we must make sure that every pupil—gifted and talented, struggling or just average—reaches the limits of their capability" (Department for Education and Skills, 2005, 20). White (2006, p. 142) also identifies such IQism, and ideas about fixed intelligence as underpinning the New Labour *Gifted and Talented Programme*. "The Gifted and Talented initiative can be seen as the latest manifestation of Galton's project, taken up by Terman, Burt and many others, of identifying an intellectual elite and making educational provision for them." Also, as noted above, racialized minorities are subjected to other aspects of policy in ways that represent them as "naturally" "dangerous" or deficient, or in terms of what Ladson-Billings (2009, p. 19) calls "marginalised and de-legitimated categories of blackness" which together, as she puts it "sculpt the extant terrain of possibilities".

Gillborn's work is also very pertinent here in the way he carefully traces a complex set of linkages in contemporary education policy, between intelligence, individualism, the management of the population, threats posed by dangerous others, the population as a resource and neo-liberalism, in relation to what he calls "degenerate discourses". He notes for example that "December 2008 also saw a slew of headlines *attacking* poor whites as a threatening and degenerate presence" (see below) (Gillborn, 2010b, p. 7). Again the relation between degeneracy, heredity and racism, which Foucault explores (2003, pp. 316–317), and was discussed previously, is very much in evidence, although Gillborn (2010b) goes on to argue that this also places the white working class in a complex relation to racialized minorities as the supposed new "race victims"—"breaks" are made at different points. He also focuses on two particular "cases" which point to "the construction of a moral panic asserting the dangers posed by a growing 'underclass' whose personal lack of responsibility and effort was asserted as the cause of 'educational failure' (among other things) and where the obvious solution is to reform tax laws (benefiting the middle class) and reduce social assistance (disciplining the working class)" (p. 17). Family, culture and blood, and security, territory and population are tightly intertwined here and are articulated again in relation to "the population-wealth problem" in a number of ways, ranging from immigration policy, to welfare and tax reform, to sex, reproduction, gender and family responsibility. As Gillborn notes: "predictably the women in the cases are singled out for special attention, with open revulsion at a woman 'churning out' children following sex with different men" (p. 17). Outrage is expressed at the intersection of the body and the city (specifically "the estate"), and of discipline and regulation, when hygiene, sexuality and degeneracy escape the effects of power. So Tyler (2006, p. 28) argues that: "The chav mum represents a thoroughly dirty and disgusting ontology that operates as the constitutive limit for the clean white middle class feminine respectability." The middle class is the "human ordinary" (Apple & Pedroni, 2005, p. 100), the chav is the "polluting other" (Apple, 2006, p.158). Here again we are skirting on the limits of humanity and bodies as objects of disgust (Ahmed, 2004). This is again the realm of abnormality, of lepers—and the ways in which racism, in Foucault's sense of "breaks in the species", functions not so much as "the prejudice or defense of one group against another as the detection of all those within a group who may be the carriers of a danger to it" (Foucault, 2003, p. 317)—in relation to whom society must be defended. I return to Gillborn's point about the role of neo-liberalism in all of this in the following chapter.

The fears surrounding degeneracy and contamination are managed in other ways in recent forms of education policy. For example, the neo-liberal logic of parental choice offers to resourceful and well-resourced parents a form of micro-social defense—enabling them to avoid "contamination" and untoward social mixes, and maintain distances "that need to be kept" (Bourdieu, 1986, p. 472) in order to maintain a "pure community", and to assuage threats to privilege and opportunity (Vincent, 2012). Choice reinstates patterns of differential access to opportunity, and establishes "breaks" through a new mechanism of responsibility.

4. "Remove the bias towards inclusion" 2.46 (p. 51) (Green paper: "Support and Aspiration: a new approach to special educational needs and disability" [Department for Education, 2011])

In "The New Division", chapter 8 of *Madness and Civilization* (2001b), Foucault outlines a set of struggles and disputes around the demarcation of categories of prisoners in eighteenth century France—paupers, libertines, villains, indigents, and the mad—in relation to their proper place in or out of society and their relation to one another. These struggles, he writes, were often conducted in "whispers" and "half-silence". He goes on to describe the "liberation" of madness and the "abolition of constraint", and their replacement by "therapeutic interventions" and "self-restraint", observation and classification, authority and reason[3]. We might discuss the liberation of "special needs" or the "feeble minded child" in the same way. The point I want to draw from this, and the continuing relevance of this analysis is that the boundaries of exclusion and the divisions between categories of normal and abnormal, special and regular are continually struggled over (as many analysts have catalogued) (Armstrong, 2009; Slee, 2011), not in any kind of linear progressive sense, but in relation to contingencies and "effects". The divisions of "ability"—physical and intellectual—and what is "normal" are unstable. They are struggled over and re-worked in a changing nexus of economics, politics and professional authority. They are embedded in struggles over language and practices, over what is "special", what is inclusion and over "appropriate" forms of provision. "Knowledge follows advances of power, discovering new objects of knowledge over all the surfaces on which power is exercised" (Foucault, 1979, p. 204) and thus "The history of psy ... is intrinsically linked to the history of government" (Rose, 1998, p. 11). Thus, Rausch (2012) describes the Warnock Report, which place an emphasis on 'mainstreaming' students with 'special needs' (Warnock, 1978) as "updating and patching onto existing flawed structures" (p. 11) and Barton and Armstrong (2007) argue that "the history of the notion of 'special educational needs' is a fine example of the complexities and contradictions involved in imposing new discourses on deeply rooted traditions and practices" (p. 9) and (Slee, 1997) reminds us of the power of "professional resilience" (p. 407). This history and our educational present looks very much like Rorty's (1982) rendering of genealogy as "reinterpretation[s] of our predecessors' reinterpretation[s] of their predecessors' reinterpretations" (p. xlii). That is, a *history* of "divergence and marginal elements" (Foucault, 1984) and relational changes, tinged with "absurdity" (Prado, 1995, p. 42).

A recent absurdity can be found in the UK Coalition Government's Green Paper *Support and Aspiration: A New Approach to Special Educational Needs and Disability*. This is a case in point of the discussion above; it signals the re-emergence of a prevailing medicalized and economistic discourse of abnormalities (1.10 to 1.17 [pp. 30–31, 5.3, p. 93]—among other things, linking SEN to Health & Wellbeing Boards through Joint Strategic Needs Assessments[4]), and once more articulates SEN as a deficit. "Other"ness is re-inscribed into policy and as Allan (2008, p. 40) puts it: "difference is continuously verified and valorised and the individuals upon whom inclusion is to be practiced are marked out with a special status." The Green Paper also suggests the need to "tackle the practice of over-identification" (p. 58)—this will be achieved by replacing the current "graduated approach" advocated by the SEN Code of Practice with a single school-based SEN category—suggesting that fewer children will be identified as "having" SENs (3.44, p. 68). There is then on the one hand, too much SEN, too many children as identified with SENs, but nonetheless, on the other, it remains in policy as a "real" deficit. What is needed is a more precise and decisive, more "scientific", categorization of abnormality—who is, who is not and what sort! The Paper also articulates with other aspects of policy, as above, for example in its problematization of parents and families—3.55 (p. 70)—especially in relation to behaviour and school exclusions.

Here again there is the interplay between classifications and exclusions, which are in turn constructed within policy in the interplay of discipline and regulation, practices and knowledges, procedures of identification and division, and institutionalized discursive systems—the "messy interactions of power and knowledge" (Olssen, 1993, p. 165). In the Green Paper and elsewhere divisions are "fabricated in piecemeal fashion" (Foucault, 1984a, p. 142) from "the errors, the false appraisals, and the faulty calculations that gave birth to those things that continue to exist and have value for us" (p. 146). The overburdened "defective child" of the nineteenth century is reproduced and continuously refined in twenty-first century education policy in an odd unstable nexus of medicine, psychology, pedagogy and law. That is to say, "the subject who knows, the objects to be known and the modalities of knowledge must be regarded as so many effects of these fundamental implications of power/knowledge and their historical transformations" (Foucault, 1979, pp. 27–28).

A General Grid of Intelligibility?

As noted in Chapter 2, Armstrong (2003) is correct in pointing out that the technologies of the eugenics movement have been employed, "on the margins of society, confronting the perceived threat to the rationality of social order" (p. 16) and that "the principle of 'normalisation', by contrast, advocated a more inclusive approach … [and] extended systems of monitoring and control to larger numbers of children and their families". However, normalization and exclusion, articulated together in relation to the limits of normality, related to fears of degeneracy and contamination, are embedded in discourses of nature and blood. These are played out and are deeply embedded in the everyday practices of contemporary, mainstream schooling and in ordinary classrooms, and are constantly reiterated and reworked in policy and legislation, in relation to the imperatives of the population as a resource.

The lines and limits and practices produced within discipline and regulation are also linked to issues of *distribution* both in terms of cost and cost-effectiveness and opportunity and interest. The discourses and practices of individualizing and totalizing both generate and "explain" these distributions—or displace them into things like parental choice or parenting capabilities or the deficit child. That is, "we seek explanation for children's failure, disengagement, distraction, anger and defiance in their genetic and medical profiles" (Slee, 2011, p. 151). Eugenics, psychologies of intelligence and the sociology of education all contribute to these displacements, locating patterns of distribution in the intellect, the home, community, or the inefficiencies of the school—rendering the discourses and practices themselves virtually invisible and their classifications neutral.

In thinking about these things I reread Nikolas Rose's discussion of exclusion in his book *The Powers of Freedom* (1999), and was struck by the aptness of the term he employs—borrowing in turn from Judith Butler, but without the psychoanalytic resonances—*abjection*. It seems to me that what I have sought to adumbrate here is a view of education as abjection. "Abjection" Rose says "is an act of force" (1999, p. 253), a "casting off or a casting down", a "demotion from a mode of existence". He also refers to "the works of division that act upon persons and collectivities such that some ways of being, some forms of existence are cast into a zone of shame, disgrace or debasement" and are "denied the warrant of tolerability, accorded a purely negative value" (p. 253); like those whom William Beveridge described in 1905 as "mere parasites". This is what we see in the primary and secondary classrooms reported above, and what I described as "economies of pupil worth", and in the exclusion of black students, and in the ideological work of the Bell-Curve, and in the recurrent remaking of "others" who are "special", but in all too deficient ways. As Rose puts it: "The political doctrines of universal citizenship do not in themselves eliminate the demand that a boundary be drawn between those who can and those who cannot be citizens" (1999, p. 254). That is, the demarcation of what Dean (2007) calls "subpopulations", a focus on which has "scratched new lines of hierarchy, authority, obligation and exception across the putatively inclusive domestic surface of liberal societies" (p. 196). And this has a particular and continuing relevance to the "problem" of "the urban" which was explored earlier. Wilson (2007) outlines the emergence of what he calls "crystallised zones of human discard", as apparatuses for "isolating" and "warehousing" black ghetto populations in US cities, zones which are deemed "cancerous to real estate sub-markets" and dangerous to the "health" of the nation (p. 6).

What I am trying to grasp at here are modes of thought, practices and forms of ethics, which focus upon and produce modern educational bodies. These elements converge upon the black body, the disabled body and the "underclass" body in both dramatic and mundane ways, set within "a regulated and polymorphous incitement to discourse" (Foucault, 1981, p. 34). They flow within and organize classroom processes and thinking. The work of nature, culture, blood and the meta-body together "expose a body totally imprinted by history" (Foucault, 1984a, p. 83)—a residual body, a discarded and abject body cast into a field of whispers and half-silences, as neither productive nor docile. In this, the school is a "precision instrument", an "analytical space" in which to "locate individuals" or from which to exclude them, it is both a normalizing and excluding machine, which draws upon and ramifies "breaks in the species". On the other side of compulsion and the universalization of education is "the antiquity and ubiquity" (Slee, 2011, p. 150) of fear, of contamination, and of eradication.

Genealogy—The 'Science of Freedom'

Where I have got to with this critique amounts to no more than a clumsy sketch, a gesture towards a different kind of education policy analysis, what Foucault calls an "anti-science", one that seeks an escape from the normative framework of liberal democracy, and from what Dean (2007) calls "our" (social and human sciences) (and my) "intimate relations" with liberalism (p. 199). There is a lot to give up. This is "a contingent history of history" (Foucault, 1983c, p. 201). It is a history of objectifying trends and subjectifying practices— (although the emphasis in this chapter has been on objectifying, the following chapter gives more attention to subjectifying). I have tried to join up some moments and events as an exercise in effective history education, to dissociate others *and to use* "Foucault's concepts [to] create new options for thought and new possibilities for action" (Rabinow & Rose, 2003 p. xi) to create a space within which it might be possible to begin to think differently about schooling (see Slee, 2011, Chapter 8 as an example, and Chapter 4). If we take Foucault seriously we must confront the problem of standing outside our own history, outside of ourselves, and do ethical work on ourselves (see Allan, 1999, p. 126). Perhaps we must cease to celebrate the creation of state schooling and see it instead as an "inglorious moment" in the "modern play of coercion over bodies" (Foucault, 1979, p. 191)?

4

HOW NOT TO BE GOVERNED
IN THAT WAY?

My objective … has been to create a history of the different modes by
which, in our culture, human beings are made subjects.

(Foucault, 1982, p. 208)

I want to address three things in this chapter each of which
is complex and all of which are interrelated. These are subjectivity, neo-liberalism and ethics. The last will also involve a brief
discussion of resistance and freedom and will take up the question of "re-writing the self" signaled in the previous chapters.
This latter is an attempt to respond to the "challenge" of
Foucault's work *and think about where the "dangers" and "costs"
outlined below and their analyses, position the academic subject.*
In part these are things which are left over from previous
chapters, things I deliberately, heuristically, delayed attending to.

They also take up again the application of Foucault to history, which was begun in the previous two chapters. That is to say, these things are about the history of the immediate present, about the shift from welfare to neo-liberalism (Jessop, 2002), from government to governmentality[1], from politics to ethics, from discipline to subjectivity. I also return briefly to the norm and abnormality. Again these three concerns—subjectivity, neo-liberalism and ethics—are linked together within my auto-biography, they relate to things that seem to me to be "cracked", and that are very clearly the "main dangers" within my every-day practice. They are about what I do and who I am now—in a dual sense—as a scholar and as a worker in the knowledge economy (see Slee & Allan, 2008, p. 45), and they indicate the ways in which I both struggle against and am constantly enfolded into neo-liberalism. What I write here is my attempt to understand these things and at the same time to come to a better understanding of Foucault's late and last work, that is the ways in which I/we are subjects in relation to new practices of governmentality and the ways in which we might struggle to escape or engage those practices.

To recap, the term *governmentality*, which Foucault once referred to as an "ugly word", and which had in the 1950s been used by Barthes, indicates a field of study which seeks knowledge about "the particular mentalities, arts and regimes of government and administration that have emerged since 'early modern' Europe" (Dean, 1999, p. 2). In more general terms, *government* is "any relatively calculated practice to direct categories of social agent to specified ends" (Dean, 1991, p. 12) or as it is often described, the "conduct of conduct" (Foucault, cited in Gordon, 1991, p. 2). It is something broader and more varied than those powers that might be said to be held by the state. It involves "a plurality of agencies and authorities, of aspects of behaviour to be governed, of norms invoked, of purposes sought, and of effects, outcomes and consequences" (Dean, 1999, p. 10) or in other words it defines a discursive field within which the exercise of power is "rationalised". *It refers not to forms of domination but technologies of government that may lead to a state of domination.*

In addressing this I will expand upon the relationships signalled by Gillborn (2010b), as quoted in the previous chapter, and then go on to say some things about the ways in which "the neo-liberal dream of competitive individualism … guides our educational consciousness and sensibilities" (Slee, 2011, p. 151). That is, the emergence of a new kind of individualism that draws upon "character" and worth to explain and justify inequalities, that constructs its own particular subjectivities, and that insinuates itself into our ethical practices. I will return to some of my previous work on *performativity* as a way of demonstrating this "consciousness and sensibilities" at work.

Subjectivity

Let us begin by repositioning the discussion in relation to Foucault's intellectual trajectory outlined in Chapter 1. Although, as noted before there is a danger and a degree of pointlessness in trying to tidy Foucault into neat stages and breaks. Nonetheless, in conventional terms this chapter draws upon Foucault's second and third *series* of lectures. The second series on political economy and governmentality (Foucault, 2009, 2004b) and the third on the ethics and aesthetics of the self (Foucault, 2010b, 1992) which were focused on the question of who we are and who we might become; that is on *askesis* and "the labour of becoming" (Venn & Terranova, 2009, p. 3). As I will try to show as we go along, the second and third series are closely interrelated and the theme of power cuts across them—they are both concerned with an intensification of power. On the one hand, the focus on subjectivity and neo-liberalism in the second series marks a shift of emphasis away from discipline and normalization that were the primary focus of the two previous chapters. On the other hand, in what follows, various continuities in Foucault's work are evident, in the redeployment of ideas introduced and developed in earlier work, and the focus on things like the body, health, division and exclusion, and nature. Nealon's Table (2008, p. 45) (Figure 4.1) is useful here in summarizing the themes, problems and displacements that cut across Foucault's work.

In the first of the last lectures, *The Courage of Truth 1983–1984*, Foucault drew together the three major themes or phases in his work—knowledge (truth), power (government) and the subject—and argued that "neither are reduced one to the other nor absorbed one by the others, but whose relations are constitutive of one another" (cited in Flynn, 2005, p. 262). He explains his "history of thought" as a history of "focal points of experience", the persistently occurring ways in which humans conceive and perceive themselves—as mad, diseased, sexual, and so forth. These focal points are studied along three axes: the axis of knowledge, or the rules of discursive practices; the axis of power; and the axis of ethics (Foucault, 2010b, pp. 1–5).

These axes and the shifts and intensifications to which they are subject, particularly in recent times, involve a repositioning and reconsideration of two social formations key to Foucault's previous analyses—the welfare state and the nation state. These shifts and intensifications, embedded in the development of

Century of Emergence	17th	17th–18th	18th–19th	19th–present
Modes of Power	Sovereign	Social	Discipline	Biopower
Primary Actor	King	Jurist	Expert	Individual
Primary Target	Flesh	Signs	Capacities	Lives
Primary Hinge	Bodies	Souls	Training	Governmentality
Primary Practice	Ceremony	Representation	Exercise	Norm
Most Intense form	Torture	Reform	Panopticism	Sexuality
Desired Outcome	Obedience	Community	Docility	Autocontrol

Figure 4.1 Foucault's Displacements 2.

governmentality, also speak very directly to our "today", and to the multiform, "heterogeneous and indistinct" (Dean, 2007, p. 91) nature of power ranging from the ontological work of neo-liberalism, to the post 9/11 proliferation of "technologies of security" (e.g. Dillon & Lobo-Guerrero, 2008). While *governmentality* will be the focus in this discussion, as Dean points out: "it is important not to telescope contemporary politics and power into questions of government" (2007, p. 91).

Government is done alongside and in relation to other modes of power but equally the other, "older" forms of power are not the same as they were in the past. In Foucault's later work, this attention to the diversity of power can be read as a more decisive move to dispositif or to "a 'topological approach' that recognizes 'patterns of correlations' and the strategic disposition of heterogeneous elements that constitute societies as particular realities" (Venn & Terranova, 2009, p. 5). That is, the fitting together of disparate techniques, processes, practices and relationships within a regime of truth to form a grid of power which operates in many different ways from many different points (Foucault, 2010a, p. 19).

What I am going to do then is briefly introduce subjectivity and some differences in Foucault's engagement with it, then "ground" this within the specificities of neo-liberalism, then "ground" both subjectivity and neo-liberalism within the "methods" of performativity, and then return to the issue of subjectivity again in relation to ethics and to resistance and to "writing the self". As we progress here we must confront very directly in different ways another of the productive paradoxes that run through Foucault's analytical work. That is, the attention given to domination and production, to liberation and enslavement, together, at the same time. He says:

> Thought is no longer theoretical. As soon as it functions it offends or reconciles, attracts or repels, breaks, dissociates, unites or reunites; it cannot help but liberate or enslave. Even before prescribing, suggesting a future, saying what must be done, even before exhorting or merely sounding an alarm, thought, at the level of its existence, in its very dawning, is in itself an action—a perilous act.
>
> (Foucault, 1977b, p. 5)

In Foucault's writing on subjectivity there are two distinct points of emphasis, the first is typically represented in his argument that there are two meanings to the word "subject": "subject to someone else by control and dependence, and tied to his own identity by a conscience or self-knowledge. Both meanings indicate a form of power which subjugates and makes subject to" (Foucault, 1982, p. 212). Here, particularly in the latter sense, "personal" qualities such as self-esteem and empowerment, as well as our hopes and dreams, fantasies and desires are artefacts of power. Subjectivity is the possibility of lived experience within a context—political and economic. Subjectivity is thus "the real basis of the self as both agent and object" (McGushin, 2011, p. 129) and enables the identities which we claim, and these identities are historically contingent. We are made up, constituted, within this double bind. However, Foucault also argued that power is an "agonism" (1982, p. 222) that is, a relationship that is a reciprocal incitement and struggle, less a confrontation than a "permanent provocation" (p. 222), and that power is therefore exercised only over free subjects who are "faced with a field of possibilities in which several ways of behaving, several reactions and diverse comportments may be realised" (p. 221). Here then, and much more to the fore in his last sequence of work, is a different way of thinking about subjectivity and about the ways in which we give form to our lives and to ourselves. That is, the idea of subjectivity as what we do, rather than who we are, as an active *process of becoming*, as the work of "*the care of the self*". That is, an art or technology of living, a set of practices through which we establish a relationship to ourselves of self-examination and determined artfulness, and through which some possibilities of freedom may be achieved, at least temporarily. "Because we have become, we can also become different" as Mendieta (2011, p. 122) puts it. This brings into play the deployment of genealogy as a critical ontology of ourselves, as a means of confronting our own revocability. It also involves us in a different reading of Foucault (Mendieta, p. 112), one that focuses upon "the truth of freedom and the freedom of truth" (p. 123) rather than upon subjection, discipline and normalization. There is a simple logic here. If power acts upon us in and through our subjectivity, then that is where our resistance and struggle to be free should be focused. As Nealon (2008) points out there are two possible readings of Foucault's later work, as either abandonment of power or its intensification, both readings are right and it is in the struggle with the tensions between them that Foucault's life ended. He died of an AIDS-related illness in Paris on June 25, 1984.

These concerns of Foucault have not been paid much attention to by education writers, despite the obvious "educational" possibilities that they suggest, rather we have tended to be primarily concerned with the constituting and disciplinary aspects of educational experience. Besley (2005) is one of the few who does discuss the application of "the care of the self" to education, and Peters (2003) also signals the relevance of Foucault's later writing on "truth-telling" to education (See also papers in Popkewitz & Brennan, 1998).

However, for the time being I am going to leave this late (or very late) Foucault aside and return to it at the end of the chapter and concentrate meanwhile on the processes he called *assujettissement*, which is usually translated as subjectivation. The point here is that there is no individual, no self, that is ontologically prior to power. There is no subject that is already formed. Subjects are produced in three interrelated modes. Firstly, as touched upon in Chapters 2 and 3, within those modes of inquiry that give themselves the status of sciences and which objectivize the speaking subject (e.g. Linguistics) or the productive subject (Economics) or the sheer fact of being alive (Biology); secondly, which was the focus of Chapters 2 and 3, those "dividing practices" that separate subjects inside themselves or from others (the mad from the sane, the sick from the healthy, the criminals from the good) and, in so doing, objectivize them; and, thirdly, the "way a human being turns him- or herself into a subject" (Foucault, 1982, p. 208); for example, how people have learned to recognize themselves as subjects of sexuality or as enterprising subjects. These modes combine and correlate within the methods of what Foucault calls *government*—using the term in its older rather than modern sense, as referring broadly to guidance for the family and for children, management of the household, directing the soul, etc.—which thus includes in its remit the government of the self and also raises the questions "[h]ow to govern oneself, how to be governed, how to govern others ..." (Foucault, 1997b, p. 97). As Dean (1999, p. 14) neatly explains "our understanding of ourselves is linked to the ways in which we are governed".

> While many forms of contemporary critique still rely on the dualism of freedom and constraint, consensus and violence, from the perspective of governmentality the polarity of subjectivity and power ceases to be plausible: government refers to a continuum, which extends from political government right through to forms of self-regulation, namely "technologies of the self". This theoretical stance allows for a more complex analysis of neo-liberal forms of government

> that feature not only direct intervention by means of empowered and
> specialised state apparatuses, but also characteristically develop
> indirect techniques for leading and controlling individuals.
>
> (Lemke, 2000, p. 12)

Essentially, within all of this neo-liberalism is both "in here" as well as "out there" (Peck, 2003). It is "in" our heads as well as "in" the economy. I want to take up governmentality and subjectivity and explore them a little further in relation to neo-liberalism. Currently, it can be said, the reciprocal relations that exist between the state and subjectivity, what we call neo-liberalism, is the "unsurpassable horizon of the age" (Dean, 1999, p. 199).

Neo-liberalism

In the lecture series *The Birth of Biopolitics 1978–1979* (2010a) Foucault took his analytic work in a particular and, for him, rather unusual direction. In these lectures he made a dual move into an examination of a specific political economy and a concomitant subjectivity and their relations—that is a focus on liberalism. He thus gave a new inflection to the notion of biopolitics. He says "Only when we know what this govern-mental regime called liberalism was, will we be able to grasp what biopolitics is" (2010a, p. 22). This is virtually the only time in his research, as opposed to his political activities, that he addressed the present directly, although he does this through a long genealogy of liberalism from the "new art of government in the eighteenth century" (p. 27) via German ordo-liberalism and Hayek, to contemporary American neo-liberalism. Again this plays upon a number of paradoxes, positioning neo-liberalism as a politics of "not governing too much" but which at the same time has been able to extend the economic form of the market "to the entire social body and to generalise it inside the whole social system that, normally, does not pass through or is not authorised by the market" (p. 248). In his course summary he described liberalism as "polymorphic" (p. 320), as both about "how not to govern too much" (p. 13) and the "present" reform and rationalization of governmentality (p. 320)—that is, how to govern differently. Furthermore, as a "mode of enquiry" neo-liberal economics is set in an antagonistic relation to the state, but at the same time neo-liberal practice is engaged in a sometimes unstable but "constant reciprocity" (p. 169) with the state (see Ball, 2012). The role of the state is "as an ensemble of apparatuses constituting both the conditions for neoliberal market capitalism and the new type of individual appropriate to it" (Venn & Terranova, 2009, p. 6). The state constructs the conditions of possibility for the economy as a "concrete and real space in which the formal structure of competition could function" (Foucault, 2010a, p. 132). That is, the economy is an ensemble of "regulated" activities, which is constantly instituted and reordered (Lazzarato, 2009), and supported and modified by the state. As before, as with madness and delinquency, new objects and subjects are produced in the "conjunctions of a whole set of practices from the moment they become coordinated with a regime of truth" (Foucault, 2010a, p. 19)—a truth that is articulated by the economy and the state together. This conjunction of practices, what we call neo-liberalism, makes "what does not exist ... become something ..." (p. 19), something that is "imperiously" marked out in reality.

Neo-liberalism is a rationality of government that relies in very particular ways on a "political anatomy of the body".

performative

This is a new iteration of the population as a resource within which individuals, institutions and states must be "lean", "fit" and flexible, and indeed agile—active citizens in an active society. "The discourse of agility is firmly rooted in neo-liberal ideology and is recognizable as a form of governance, a contemporary governmentality which promises to 'shape the conduct of diverse actors without shattering their formally autonomous character (Miller & Rose, 2008, p. 39)' (Gillies, 2011, p. 219). Or as Vander Schee (2009) puts it: "individuals are provided the opportunity for consummate involvement in the administration of their own lives" (p. 558). Again not all of this may be "bad" or "worse" but it is "dangerous". Here bodies are not just "docile" rather they are engaged in a form of insidious "disciplined self-management" (Ozga, 2009, p. 152) which involves making themselves healthy, "ready", adaptable and agentic in relation to the needs of fast capitalism, while at the same time, as "biological citizens", taking responsibility for the damage that capital does to them. This is "a re-coding of social mechanisms of exploitation and domination on the basis of a new topography of the social" (Lemke, 2000, p. 14). The move from the welfare state to the neo-liberal state involves a redistribution of responsibilities and the emergence of new forms of government—self-government. "Activism and responsibility have now become … part of the obligation of the … biological citizen. Such a citizen is obliged to inform himself … about susceptibilities and predispositions …[and] to take appropriate steps…in the name of the minimization of illness and the maximization of health" (Rose & Novas, 2004, p. 402–403).

Life is made meaningful and of value "to the extent that it can be rationalised as the outcome of choices made or to be made" (Rose, 1996, p. 57). Empowerment and obligation go hand in hand. Through the calculative techniques of the self-help manual, of coaching, counselling, mentoring, etc. we turn "the gaze" upon ourselves to see if we "add-up", we audit ourselves, make ourselves "experts of ourselves" (Rose, 1996). We learn about ourselves, and self-confess through hybridized, psychologically-based knowledges. Such knowledge is the priority as we strive to live up to "perfection codes" of mind and body—although this is clearly a classed and gendered "we".

It is not that "initiative", "enterprise", "responsibility" or "activity" are not worthwhile human capacities. ... Rather, it is that within the frame of entrepreneurial selfhood ... [they] are narrowly imagined in relation to the performance of exchange relations in the extended order of capitalist markets.

(Kelly, 2006, p. 29)

The argument is that the insidious economisation of the social consistent with marketised relations has become such a pervasive process that subjectivity itself is held fast within its matrix, creating the problem of finding unterritorialised spaces for practices of resistance.

(Venn & Terranova, 2009, p. 4)

Neo-liberalism is realized in practical relations of competition and exploitation within business but also in very mundane and immediate ways in our institutions of everyday life, and thus it "does us"—speaks and acts through our language, purposes, decisions and social relations. In thinking about these practices, and concomitant changes in the form and modalities of the state, we can also think about how we are "reformed" by neo-liberalism, and made into different kinds of educational workers or learners. At its most visceral and intimate neo-liberalism involves the transformation of social relations and practices into calculabilities and exchanges, that is into the market form—with the effect of commodifying educational practice and experience. Neo-liberalism is made possible by a "new type of individual", an individual formed within the logic of competition—a calculating, solipsistic, instrumentally driven, "enterprise man". This is a "remoralisation" of our relation to the state and to ourselves (Peters, 2001, pp. 59–60) in as much that: "It aspires to construct a responsible and moral individual ... whose moral quality is based on the fact that they rationally assess the costs and benefits of a certain act..." (Lemke, 2000, p. 12). The research on parental choice, for example, exemplifies this kind of responsible and assiduous individualism in contemporary education (see Vincent, 2012). The responsible parent calculates the relation of choices now to the shaping of the future lives of their children. This is the ontology of neo-liberalism: "... the only real agents, must be individuals, or let's say, if you like enterprises" (Foucault, 2010a, p. 173). The individual, the institution, our social relations become modelled on, microcosms of, the business, organized upon "the individual's function, as a molecular fraction of capital" (Lazzarato, 2009, p. 121). This is "a reconceptualisation of life itself" (Venn & Terranova, 2009). Neo-liberal governmentalities work "to produce healthy, productive and flexible populations" (Edwards, 2002), populations with "the ability to profit from continuous pedagogic reformations" (Bernstein, 2001a, p. 365), which rest in turn on the forgetting of prior habits, and a commitment to "de-learning" (Bauman, 2004, p. 22) for the duration of life—lifelong learning. In effect what is being constructed is a new ontology of learning and of policy and a very elaborate "technology of the self" through which we shape our bodies and subjectivities to the needs of learning, "developing not only a 'sense' of how to be, but also 'sensibility': requisite feelings and morals…" (Colley, James et al., 2003, p. 471). The lifelong learner exists within a new moral environment (Haydon, 2004) inside of which values, social relations and self-worth are tightly tied to the imperatives of an enterprising life and "enterprise is positioned as a principle of the 'good life'" (Edwards, 2002, p. 357). Indeed, "the 'economic politics' of Enterprise appears to know no boundaries either in terms of where it might be applied" (du Gay, 2004, p. 40) or to whom. Inside these policies we are "sentencing learners to life" (Falk, 1999). That is, we are moving inexorably towards "the learning society", a society in which "every adult possess(s) a personal learning plan, written down and monitored with a chosen mentor; every organisation seek(s) to become a learning organisation" (Keep, 1997, p. 457). In Bernstein's terms (2001a) these are the outlines of a "totally pedagogised society" and the "pedagogisation of life" in which learning is an activity that is conducted endlessly, "in which the State is moving to ensure that there's no space or time which is not pedagogised" (Bernstein, 2001a, p. 377). The recurring issue is "whether an increase in our capabilities must necessarily be purchased at the price of our intensified subjection" (Burchell, 1996, p. 34).

More generally, as Lazzarato| (2009) suggests, neo-liberalism rests upon five states of being, which interrelate and interdepend: individualization, inequality, insecurity, depoliticization and financialization. These constitute a "politics of the social" and an ontological framework that displaces the principles of the welfare state. Very briefly: *Individualization* has been discussed above. *Inequality* is the basis for envy and striving, and competition, as Lazzarato (2009) puts it "appetites and instincts are not given: only inequality has the capacity to sharpen appetites, instincts and minds, driving individuals to rivalries" (p. 117). Nonetheless, market theorists, like Hayek, argue that these instincts are "natural". Neo-liberalism incites us to compete, and thus Lazzarato says, it "consumes freedom" (p. 120). *Insecurity* is the basis for both responsibility and enterprise. We must take responsibility for our own needs and for our well-being, as above, and for dealing with risk and uncertainty and organizing protection from them, we can no longer rely on the state (see O'Malley, 1996, on prudentialism). We are made fearful and therefore active, neo-liberalism produces what Lazzarato (2009 p. 120) calls "a micro-politics of little fears". This is an "affective" basis for government. Precarity is a fundamental condition of neo-liberal society. Our emotions are linked to the economy through our anxieties and our concomitant self-management (as above) and the state becomes the site of minimal provision and last resort (Foucault, 2010a, p. 149). *Depoliticization* acts in parallel to this, sometimes rendering collective conditions of experience into personal problems, sometimes displacing political and economic decisions into individual failings and responsibilities (see also Hall, 1989; Apple, 2012). Finally, *Financialization* is pertinent in a number of ways. For example, in translating the security of work and state pensions into personal investments with attendant risks, while at the same time rendering us into savers and shareholders, blurring the distinction between wage-earner and capitalist, as we all become dependent directly or indirectly on the regimes of banking and investment. Thus, we must calculate ourselves in another sense in relation to an uncertain future. Concomitantly the tax burden is shifted "away from corporations towards individual wage earners" (Peters, 2001, p. 59). This "splits each person internally into a 'schizophrenic' double, torn by the different, possibly opposite rationalities" (Lazzarato 2009 p. 125). This interrelates again with *individualization* and *depoliticization*. We can also think of these processes as a form of what Harvey (2005) calls "accumulation by dispossession", by which he means the redistribution of public or commonly held assets and resources, through colonization, privatization and financialization, as private property. This has the effect of fragmenting and particularizings social conflicts. Collective interests are replaced by competitive relations and it becomes increasingly difficult to mobilize workers around issues of general significance. Collective professional values are displaced by commercial values, and professionals are dispossessed of their expertise and judgment. *Financialization* is also evident in a variety of ways in new relations between the state and capital, among which is the opening up of state services to the logics of profit and competition (see Ball, 2012). The state makes itself into an opportunity for profit, **and** seeks to reform itself in the image of the market (see below). Furthermore, in this process of auto-reform, as noted above, the state changes the boundaries and definitions of what the economy is and what the state is. Governmentality is "at once internal and external to the state, since it is the tactics of government which make possible the continual definition and redefinition of what is within the competence of the state and what is not" (Gordon, Miller et al., 1991, p. 103). Within all of this, in the twenty-first century, the costs of managing the population are reworked and redistributed as the state "out-sources" its disciplinary systems to systems of enterprise, dismantling at the same time the structures of power/ knowledge and specifically the professions which were the bulwarks of older forms of disciplinary government (Chapter 2). All five of these aspects and foundations of neo-liberalism are very evident within almost all parts contemporary higher education, to a greater or lesser extent, and indeed in different ways in all and every other form of contemporary education (Ball, 2012), and are particularly evident in what I have called, with due deference to Lyotard (1984) and Butler (1990), the methods of *performativity*. I am going to take Higher Education as a case in point.

Re-visiting Performativity: Living the Neo-Liberal University

> ... at what cost is the truth of individuals spoken when, say, its condition and effect is their efficient disciplinary subjection?
>
> (Burchell, 1996, pp. 33–34)

> The real political task in a society such as ours is to criticize the workings of institutions that appear to be both neutral and independent, to criticize and attack them in such a manner that the political violence that has always exercised itself obscurely through them will be unmasked, so that one can fight against them.
>
> (Chomsky, Foucault et al., 2006, p. xx)

The essential point about performativity is that we must make ourselves calculable rather than memorable. In regimes of performativity, experience is nothing, productivity is everything. Last year's efforts are a benchmark for improvement— more publications, more research grants, more students. We must keep up; strive to achieve the new and ever more diverse targets which we set for ourselves in appraisal meetings; confess and confront our weaknesses; undertake appropriate and value-enhancing professional development; ensuring what O'Flynn and Petersen (2007, p. 469) call a "targeted self" or what Gee (1999) refers to as the "shape-shifting portfolio person". *Performativity* is a key mechanism of neo-liberal government that uses comparisons and judgements, and self-management, in place of interventions and direction. Within all of this more and more of the scholarly disposition is rendered explicit and auditable, the subject of and to new "truths" and visibilities, to a "ruthless curiosity". As Venn and Terranova (2009) suggest "the 'life' of markets becomes increasingly indexed, formalised and virtualised by means of mathematical formalisations; additionally, it is also concretely actualised in the form of serial acts of communication … the market itself becomes both more abstract and machinic … 'cold' and 'calculating'…" (p. 9)—our days are numbered, literally! Here economic exploitation takes the form of a "political investment of the body" (Foucault, 1977a, p. 25), or in the knowledge economy a political investment in both mind and body; both as throughput—more students and teaching hours—and as output, that is intellectual productivity and the harnessing of this output more directly to economic exploitation—to "impact" and commercial exploitation. This brings about a commodification of the researcher. Performativity is enacted through indicators and targets against which we are expected to position ourselves but often in ways that also produce uncertainties about how we should organize ourselves within our work—we work as Bauman terms it in "the age of contingency" (Bauman, 1996), within "new diagrams of force and freedom" (Rose, 1996, p. 55). A consequence of continual animation and calculation is for many a growing sense of ontological insecurity; both a loss of a sense of meaning in what we do and of what is important in what we do. Shore and Wright (1999) even go far as to suggest, that these uncertainties are a tactic for the destabilization of the public sector. We are in danger of becoming transparent but empty, unrecognizable to ourselves—"I am other to myself precisely at the place where I expect to be myself" (Butler, 2004, p. 15).

Increasingly, as we adapt ourselves to the challenges of reporting and recording our practice, interpersonal social structures and social relations are replaced by informational structures and performance indicators become the "principle of intelligibility of social relationships". We are stood before a "permanent economic tribunal" (Foucault, 2010a) against which all intellectual activity is judged (Simons & Masschelien, 2006). Furthermore, there is an individuation of educational institutions as they compete with one another to recruit and perform, **and** of the educational workplace—with more and more short-term projects, freelancers, consultants, agency-workers, fixed-term contracts, skill-mixes—these new kinds of workers are "with" and "for" the organization, rather than "in" it (Wittel, 2001, p. 65). Social ties within educational work become ephemeral, disposable, serial, fleeting. Within this liquid, modern academic world social relations are "eminently dismantleable" (Bauman, 2004, p. 22) and are themselves a commodity—something to be "invested in", that produces "returns". Performativity then, is a "new" moral system that subverts and re-orients us to its truths and ends. It makes us responsible for our performance and for the performance of others. We are burdened with the responsibility to perform, and if we do not we are in danger of being seen as irresponsible. "There are two technologies at play here turning us into governable subjects—a technology of *agency* and a technology of *performance*" (Davies & Petersen, 2005, p. 93). We are produced rather than oppressed, animated rather than constrained. Indeed, at times, as Broadhead and Howard (1998) admit, we participate in all of this not reluctantly but "imaginatively, aggressively, and competitively". We take responsibility for working harder, faster and better as part of our sense of personal worth and our estimation of the worth of others. Being responsible and enterprising is "both a leverage for change as well as a closure on what it is possible to become" (Hatcher, 1998, p. 382). These techniques of regulation and self-regulation are creating a new *episteme* of public service through a "reshaping of 'deep' social relations" (Leys, 2001, p. 2) which involve the subordination of moral and intellectual obligations to economic ones (Walzer, 1984) so that "everything is simply a sum of value realised or hoped for" (Slater & Tonkiss, 2001). Value displaces values (Peters, 2003, p. 17), truths told about us displace our concern for truth—the risks of "truth-telling" stand over and against the costs of silence (see Tamboukou, 2012). The neo-liberal subject is malleable rather than committed, flexible rather than principled. As Tamboukou (2012) asks, in her timely discussion of Foucault's *parrhesia* (truth telling) and Arendt's *pariah*: "what is the role of the academic when going through 'dark times', vis-à-vis questions of truth telling; what are the conditions of possibility for truth telling to be recognised as a question or a problem and how can we start mapping the effects of what we as academics do or refrain from doing?" This is a question about the forms and possibilities of freedom, ethics and resistance, to which I return later.

Productive rather than truthful individuals are the new subjects and the central resource in a reformed, entrepreneurial public sector. CVs are traded in the research economy—we are headhunted (how appropriate) and sell ourselves to the highest bidder. There are a particular set of skills to be acquired here—skills of presentation and of inflation, making the most of ourselves and making a spectacle of ourselves. We seek out research funding wherever it can be found and avoid thinking about who is funding and what is being funded, we become "entrepreneurial researchers" (Ozga, 1998). Those who "underperform" are subject to moral approbation and the tyranny of "little fears". Systems designed to "support" or encourage those who are unable to "keep up" continuously teeter on the brink of moral regulation. The force and brute logic of performance and its "modest and omniscient" (Rose, 1996, p. 54) practices are hard to avoid. To do so, in one sense at least, means letting ourselves down, in terms of the logic of performance, and letting down our colleagues and our institution. This is another manifestation of "dividing practices", which work to identify, valorize and reward the successful and productive—the "affiliated" (Miller & Rose, 2008, p. 98), and to target for exile or for reform those who fail to re-make themselves in "the image of the market" (Gillies, 2011, p. 215).

Also then it is important to recognize that performative systems offer us the possibility of being better than we were or even being excellent—and better than others—in its own terms. Performativity is not in any simple sense a technology of oppressions; it is also one of satisfactions and rewards, at least for some. "The language and practices of neoliberal managerialism are seductive. They lay the grounds for new kinds of success and recognition" (Davies and Petersen, 2005, p. 1). Indeed, performativity works best when we come to want for ourselves what is wanted from us, when our moral sense of our desires and ourselves are aligned with its pleasures. In a sense it is about making the individual into an enterprise, as suggested above, a self-maximizing productive unit operating in a market of performances—committed to the "headlong pursuit of relevance as defined by the market" (Falk, 1999).

Performativity then makes a crucial contribution to the rendition of teaching and learning into calculabilities, it generates market information for choosers, enables the state to "pick off" poor performers, and makes it possible to translate educational work, of all kinds, into contracts articulated as forms of performance delivery, which can then be opened to "tender" and thus to competition from private providers by means of "contracting out". In turn, as noted already, contracts bring about a re-shaping of the culture and structures of governance (both institutional and national) and of service relationships and of the commitments of public service workers. All of this is only too perfectly exemplified by the UK Research Excellence Framework (REF), both in the ways in which it translates the rating of the worth of knowledge into specific levels of funding, and the mundane, repetitive and methodical ways in which we are daily subjected to its "swarming of disciplinary mechanisms" (Foucault, 1979, p. 211) as our scholarship and writing are carefully "geared" to the demands and prescriptions of the REF categories. As HEFCE indicates (2009, p. 8) "We will be able to use the REF to encourage desirable behaviours at three levels", including, "the behaviour of individual researchers within a submitted unit …". Indeed Olssen argues that with the REF "there is a new shift from accountability over finances to control over substance and the content of what is researched" (Olssen, 2011, p. 345). The last vestiges of the independence of universities from the state, he argues, are cast aside.

However, particularly and peculiarly, academic subjects also have a repertoire of analytic tropes and possibilities and forms of existence to draw upon which can enable us to question "what is given to us as necessary to think and do" (Burchell, 1996, p. 32), to subvert the new games of truth within which we are reworked. Spaces remain in which we might "invent or contrive new ways of saying the truth" (Blacker, 1998, p. 32). Blacker suggests that Foucault is "tailor made for intellectuals engaged in research within an institutional setting such as the contemporary university" (p. 348).

Back to Subjectivity: Ethics and Resistance and Freedom

> How can we still today in our historical present find ways of significantly clarifying and warranting the ethical-political perspectives that inform a critique of the present? This is *the* question that Foucault's genre of critique requires us to raise, a question he never quite answered.
>
> (Bernstein, 1994, pp. 234–235)

The last phase of Foucault's work is difficult, confusing and fascinating in a number of ways, although we might want to say that about all of his work. However, as indicated in Chapter 1 and above, this last phase involves both a further "intensification" of power related to previous themes and concerns and a revision of the ways in which those themes and concerns are treated. In effect Foucault rereads and reworks his earlier work in some surprising ways so that "it does appear to be the case that Foucault is suggesting that he is best read backwards rather than forwards" (Encyclopedia of Philosophy). By 1982 he had elaborated a framework for his work that grants self-constitution considerable importance and seemed to accept that his earlier work was too insistent on the formation of subjectivity by discursive practices and power-relations (Defert & Ewald, 2001, p. 177, p. 225). He indicated and explored various "ways out" of what Prado (1995, p. 46) calls his "paralyzing impasse". Thus, Besley (2005, p. 78) writes: "In his later writings he broke with this relationship to emphasise games of truth not as a coercive practice, but rather as an ascetic practice of self-formation". "Ascetic" in this context means an "exercise of self upon the self by which one attempts to develop and transform oneself, and to attain a certain mode of being" (Foucault, 1997b, p. 282). Perhaps as always Foucault himself was the exemplar for new forms of ethics and of political and academic practice, perhaps made even more urgent and pointed by his awareness at this time of the imminence of his death. Smith (2007) comments that Foucault "appeared to act out a life reflexively engaged with forming itself and the world even while describing the massive restraint on possibilities, for which the panopticon, or total institution, was a vivid symbol".

Through his work on a genealogy of "truth-telling" he comes to a view of the subject as both constituted and self-constituting in the relationships between discursive practices (that determine what counts as true or false) and power-relations (the rationalities and techniques by which one governs the conduct of others) and ethics (the practices of self through which an individual constitutes itself as a subject)[2]. Ethics here concern the kind of relation one has to oneself and indicate a different form of self government, structuring and shaping the field of possible action of subjects, the other side of the paradox of subjectivity, and a move away from docile bodies but still based on a "complementarity and conflicts between techniques which assure coercion and processes through which the self is constructed and modified by himself" (Foucault, 1993, p. 204). As Youdell (2006, p. 42) explains, Foucault's later work suggests "that the person is made subject by and subject to discursive relations of disciplinary power, but being such a subject s/he can also engage self-consciously in practices that might make her/him differently. The subject acts, but s/he acts within/at the limits of subjectivation". Sawicki (1991, p. 175) probably overstates the case somewhat when she writes about this as the "fluidity, reversibility and mutability of relations of power". Even so it is arguable whether Foucault did have time to articulate a clear position on the conceptual fit between his critique of the modern subject and his account of ethics.

Politically this last set of intellectual moves can be read in different ways. Some commentators see the focus on ethics and the care of the self as a form of nihilism. Over and against that we might see these concerns as a modern form of politics that is a response to modern forms of power, and a set of relationships between intellectual practice, self formation and political engagement. Foucault is indicating the ways in which genealogy can be put to use as a political tool and as a means of self-formation. That is, as a way of making it more difficult to act and think "as usual" and of rethinking our relationship to ourselves and to others, and our possibilities of existence. What he outlines as *askesis* is a style or attitude or practice of selfhood that will enable us "to fully confront the world in an ethical and rational manner" (Foucault, 1983a). That is, a commitment to a kind of "permanent agonism" (Burchell, 1996, p. 34).

> The critical ontology of ourselves has to be considered not, certainly, as a theory, a doctrine, nor even as a permanent body of knowledge

that is accumulating; it has to be conceived as an attitude, an ethos,
a philosophical life in which the critique of what we are is at one and
the same time the historical analysis of the limits that are imposed
on us and an experiment with the possibility of going beyond them.
(Foucault, 1984b, p. 118)

As explored previously, through his genealogical work Foucault
was seeking to render certain taken-for-granted exercises
of power "intolerable", by exposing them to scrutiny. His
point is that the exercise of power only remains tolerable by
hiding itself within the everyday, the mundane and the intimate. One task of the intellectual, but not theirs exclusively, is
to make people aware of how intolerable taken-for-granted
exercises of power actually are and show them that things
could be different. This involves analysis of and experimentation on the limits within which we are set. That is, "a certain
determination to throw off familiar ways of thought and to
looks at the same things in a different way" (Foucault, 1988a,
p. 321) and "a lack of respect for the traditional hierarchies of
what is important and fundamental" (p. 321) This involves
working on and caring for the self, and seeking what Burchell
(1996) calls "ways out" (p. 30), by developing a sense of "the
inventedness of our world" (p. 30), that is "a kind of operation
that turns the present inside out" (p. 31)—which is what
Chapters 2 and 3 were about. This involves us, as Burchell
goes on to suggest, in a "reproblematisation" of the present
that "dismantles the coordinates of his or her starting point
and indicates the possibility of a different experience" (p. 31).
This ethics of intellectual work rests on both a "concern for
truth" (p. 31) and a "concern for existence" (p. 33). The first
demands recognition of the historicity of truth, the disturbance

of conventional ways of thinking and the search for new modes and spaces and players in and rules for "the game of truth" (see Youdell and Allan below). Pignatelli (1993, p. 425) puts this very nicely when he writes about "a suppleness, an informed tentativeness that remains alert to unanticipated openings and possibilities". The second, relatedly, is the acknowledgement that "what exists does not exhaust the possibilities of existence" (Burchell, 1996, p. 34). Together these concerns draw our attention to the "costs" of the limits of possibility—what is lost, obscured, sacrificed in the present! The relations of truth and existence also demarcate the possibilities of freedom, and a particular kind of freedom. One that is not a state of being but a struggle of becoming, an endless effort of reinvention, and of struggle between capability and constraint, limitations and transgression, in order "To become again what we should have been but never were" (Foucault, 2004, p. 95). This anticipates Youdell's (2006) point below about "provisionality". What one is or might be has to be obtained by hard labour and this labour is never done. The point of this effort is: "How not to be governed in that way" (Foucault, 1997c).

To reiterate, this is another Foucault, one that reads or can be read, very differently from the Foucault represented in most uses of his work in educational studies, which tend to stress the impossibility of freeing oneself from power relations or which fails to recognize the productive nature of power. In the last and incomplete phase of Foucault's work, subjectivity, ethics, resistance and freedom are interwoven in complex (to use that word again) and multi-layered ways, philosophically grounded in Heidegger, Kant and Socrates (see Peters, 2000, 2003; Tamboukou, 2012). As noted already, Foucault begins by rejecting the modernist notion of an essential self, and of self understanding as a process of "finding" ourselves. Rather the task is to produce ourselves, to experiment, to make ourselves through practices of care. We can unsettle and we can unsettle ourselves. This goes back to the point that systems of thought, organization and practices, "what we are, what we think, and what we do today" (Foucault, 1984a, p. 32) are not as necessary as all that and can be thought differently. All of this relates back to and rests on Foucault's efforts at making the subject historically mutable and thus the possibility of "making ourselves open to transformation" (Taylor, 2011, p. 112). Foucault said in an interview "My role—and that is too emphatic a word—it's to show people that they are freer than they think" (Martin, Gutman et al., 1988, pp. 10–11). This also relates back to Foucault's interest in transgression and marginality and the recovery of "subjugated knowledges". It also links to the question of ethics, to the idea of the self to be "fashioned through vigilance, courage and perseverance so that we may be worthy of governing others" (Taylor, 2011, p. 115). This is the basis for freedom, in which freedom is "a vocation, an *asecesis*" (p. 112) and is by definition "not a state of being, but a relation to ourselves" (p. 112) within conditions of uncertainty and of ontological instability. It is also a move beyond "the idea of universal necessities of human existence" (Martin, 1988, pp. 10–11). Here freedom is never stable—it always has to be practiced, sustained and wrested. This is what Foucault called "concrete liberty" (Defert & Ewald, 2001, p. 449) a term first used in *Madness and Civilization* (Foucault, 2001b, p. 240), which arises in spaces of fragility as a reaction against the context of the moment and a specific state of affairs which we confront rather than as part of a struggle for ultimate truth (see Veyne, 2010, p. 109)—that is everyday resistance to everyday power, its proliferation and saturation, with the effect that "our modes of resistance become increasingly subtle and intense" (Nealon, 2008, p. 108). That is, "one has to start where one is, with the provocation to respond to 'today', a particular problem or set of problems, and one is forced to end with something other than a condemnation or judgement" (Nealon, 2008, p. 111). There are effects to which we have to respond but what is important here is strategic knowledge rather than abstract bodies of thought. These former are the basis of ethics and of resistance. That is to say, "For Foucault, resistance was inherent within relations of power, and resistance was itself predicated on the existence of a free subject. Resistance was not an isolated, quixotic event; rather, Foucault saw it as a means of self-transformation through the minimisation of states of domination" (Butin, 2001, p. 158).

This creates the possibility of a form of freedom framed within the limits of history. This is a further iteration of Foucault's focus on practices and their histories. And there is another play here with words, he makes the point that resistance involves both resisting practices and practices of resistance. That is, one key point of focus of resistance is against *practices*, particularly the multifarious practices of governmentality, but he is also interested in the ways in which this resistance "to" may be practiced and what it can tell us about power. That means: "taking the forms of resistance against different forms of power as a starting point … in order to understand what power relations are about, perhaps we should investigate the forms of resistance and attempts made to dissociate these relations" (Foucault, 1983d, pp. 210–211). Foucault saw struggle both as formative and informative, rather than futile: "it is only through struggling against calcified institutional and individual relations of power that resistance becomes useful" (Butin, 2001, p. 173). All of this involves constant and organized work on the self, that is, the "establishment of a certain objectivity, the development of a politics and a government of the self, and an elaboration of an ethics and practice in regard to oneself" (Foucault, 1997a). This also involves an awareness of the dangers of the present and ongoing critical reflection—this is the work of a practical rather than a metaphysical self—which can clear spaces of possibility for experimentation with new modes of existence. "Inherent in this explorative attitude is an attempt to step beyond the politically determined nature of our deepest thoughts and experiences. It logically implies the depoliticisation of experience" (http://savageriley.blogspot.co.uk/2011/11/art-zen-and-insurrection-finding.html). That is, the need to constantly interrupt oneself, to make ethico-political choices, to remain alert to the dangers which lurk in the everyday, in the "steady, persistent drone" (Pignatelli, 1993, p. 425) of the mundane and obvious, and to question the limits of what we say and how we act. "The source of human freedom" (Foucault, 1988c, p. 1) said "is never to accept anything as definitive, untouchable, obvious or immobile".

As noted earlier little of this later work has been taken up in relation to educational studies or the sociology of education, but Youdell (2006) and Allan (1999) have put some of these ideas to work in their research, in a very Foucauldian fashion. Both seek to make sense of power relations at the margins, in the interplay of norms and abnormality, and focused on the body—the intertwinement of the body "with practices of power mean that it has a central role in practices of resistance too ..." (Oksala, 2007, p. 85). In a sense they take up where the genealogies sketched in Chapters 2 and 3 leave off.

Youdell (2006) sets about applying *akesis* to education in the form of what she calls "a politics of performative reinscription" (p. 180), that is "moments of politics" in which school students make themselves and/or others "something, or someone, they were not before" (p. 180), although she also notes the "limits, risks and provisionality of such reinscription" (p. 180). She goes on to consider how such a post-structural politics might operate in school "as a site of politics" (p. 186) through educators' practices and reflexivity, in pedagogy, the curriculum, institutional practices and policy (pp. 182–185). Intriguingly, for Foucault, the teacher, although not what we now mean by the teacher, is fundamental in calling us to the care of the self (Peters, 2003). Youdell then takes up Foucault in a similar way to Allan, who in relation to inclusion in schools, explores how "pupil's transgressive practices enabled them to develop new forms of subjectivity" (Youdell, 1999, p. 105) as a kind of "gender politics" which "promoted new knowledge of their experiences as disabled, gendered and sexual subjects" (p. 108). Allan also considers how this politics might be played out, by SEN pupils, mainstream pupils, teachers, schools and researchers. The ethical work of the latter would include "examining their own role in research and the effects of the kinds of knowledge about special education which they have produced" (p. 124); which in an oblique way is what I have tried to begin to do in this book. Allan also takes seriously the aesthetics of this kind of work on the self and in relation to others, which has a particular and poignant relevance in relation to disability, and she demonstrates the relation of aesthetics to politics. Both Allan and Youdell are looking at education from the outside in, as I have also tried to do in a highly generalized way, they are viewing the present truths and forms of existence which operate within education, and their *costs*, from the perspective of those who bear the heaviest burden of those costs.

So where does all of this get us, where does it get me—what work on myself have I been able to achieve here? What kind of ethical subject is being written here and how does that relate to the sort of person I might want to be?

Rewriting the Self

> ... educational researchers must be willing to experiment with new truths. One must always bear in mind and grapple with the fact that new "regimes of truth" may replace old authoritarian principles; yet it should be realised that some forms of domination are more dangerous than others.
>
> (Butin, 2001, p. 174)

Let me be clear, this is not an exercise of confession, neither it is a claim to the achievement of self-constitution or self-mastery, or of an "aesthetics of existence", although I might claim a greater awareness, at the end of writing this, of the extent to which my academic practice was and is constituted in "games of truth" and practices of government. The processes of resistance and liberation are in part, in the modern context, processes of knowing and caring for the self.

What I have sought to do is to rewrite myself in relation to the sociology of education and education policy studies, to re-inscribe some of the lines and demarcations which cut across their practices and theories, to dismantle some of my cherished intellectual coordinates and starting points, in order to seek a different way of being a subject "of" sociology. "One's idea of what one is struggling against has a direct impact on what one becomes as one struggles" (Blacker, 1998, p. 357). Foucault saw writing as a key technique of the "arts of the self", and a means for exploring the "aesthetics of existence" and for inquiring into the government of self and others. He discussed "the role of writing in the philosophical culture of the self just prior to Christianity: its close tie with apprenticeship; its applicability to movements of thought; its role as a test of truth" (Foucault, 1997d, p. 235) and presented self-writing as a deliberate, self-conscious attempt to explain and express oneself to an audience within which one exists and from whom one seeks confirmation (see Peters, 2000). This aptly sums up what I have been attempting here, although in another sense sits uneasily with my efforts to unsettle, disconcert and discomfort myself and my readers. Perhaps the most important thing, and the point I made at the beginning of the book, is that Foucault makes me think, and in particular here I have sought to use his work to "mark out an ethical space" (Burchell, 1996, p. 34) within which I might do my intellectual practice differently and explore the possibilities and impossibilities of transgression, and have a different kind of relationship to myself as I weigh up the risks and costs of telling truths against the consequences and costs[3] of doing *not doing* so, in what seems like an increasingly one-sided "parrhesiastic game" (Foucaulta, 2001a, p. 13).

I have sought to transgress and to unsettle by beginning to write a history of the educational present, and rewrite the history of education policy—*to aim an arrow at the heart of the present*, as Habermas said of Foucault. That is, to rewrite education policy as a history of *practices, and truths and subjects, and of relations of power and of government.* I have tried to turn education policy inside out, using exclusion and abjection to think about policy rather than policy to think about exclusion, by attending to the "ignoble" history of classifications and exclusions, and to the ways of which these divisions, alongside others, set limits to the possibility of humanity. I am very aware that this is only a beginning and much more needs to be done. This has also been my strategy, in the spirit of this book series, for demonstrating the possibilities and costs that arise if we take Foucault's method seriously and seek to apply his problematizations, the examination of the ways in which things become thinkable and practicable, systematically to education policy, and it is also my answer to (Peters & Besley, 2007) question "Why Read Foucault?"

So how do I finish? Where have I got to? Or perhaps more appropriately what has not been done and what do I do next? Not for the moment knowing how to answer those questions, I shall leave the last words to Mitchell Dean and to Foucault himself.

> By becoming clear about the limits, we open up the possibility of an action to accept or reject them, to show their contingent nature, or to add up the costs of transgressing them. Above all, the point of a critical ontology of ourselves and our present is to make us clear on these risks and dangers, these benefits and opportunities, so that we might take or decline to take action.
>
> (Dean, 1999, p. 14)

> Good, well that's it. Thank you. (The end of the final lecture in the series *The Birth of Biopolitics,* Foucault, 2010a, p. 313)

NOTES

Chapter 1

1. In a question and answer session with students in the Department of History at the University of Berkeley in 1983, he was asked: "You say power is everywhere ...?" He replied, "No, power relations are everywhere".
2. Perhaps I could borrow those sentences and ask you to read them again in relation to this text!

Chapter 2

1. It important to recognize that there is a longer history to all of this as Deacon (2006, p. 121) points out "modern education emerged, almost prefabricated, from the contingent, discontinuous and interdependent material practices and imperatives of various disciplinary technologies".
2. This fourth lecture was published separately in Gordon, Miller et al. (1991) and its take-up gave impetus to what is sometimes called "*governmentality studies*" which is one of the most widespread and productive fields in which Foucault's work has been taken forward.
3. At the end of this fourth lecture Foucault adds a coda which links this new form of analysis back to the work he undertook in *The Order of Things* on the emergence of the modern human sciences—biology, economics and linguistics. He suggests that "a constant interplay between techniques of power and their object gradually carves out in reality, as a field of reality, population and its specific phenomena.

A whole series of objects were made visible for possible forms of knowledge ... " (1970b, p. 79). Specifically, the possibilities for knowledges of man; the human subject is a nineteenth century production for it is then "that human forces confront purely finitary forces—life, production, language—in such a way that the resulting composite is a form of Man" (Deleuze, 1995). Here is another point of intersection between archeology and genealogy.

4. Foucault says "racism first develops with colonisation, or in other words, with colonising genocide" (p. 257)—slavery and imperialism. Foucault's terminology collides somewhat awkwardly with more recent uses of "new racism" (e.g. Barker, 1981; Hylton, 2009).

5. By 1978 Foucault had established a distinction between *normalization*, which he then attributes solely to biopower and describes as the process of establishing the norm from different normal curves, and the disciplinary process of bringing subjects into conformity with a predetermined norm which he thence refers to as *normation*.

6. He intended to write book on this, with the tentative title 'Populations and Races'.

7. I have made little mention here of what might be called the history of menstrual blood but see for example Dyhouse (1983).

8. There is another double here, a blurring of observation and inference, of classification and measurement, of classical and modern. On the one hand, there is a visibility of types, Burt et al. used photographs to 'show' abnormality, children were made "describable"; affinities and resemblances within groups were represented in grids and tables. But alongside taxonomy, psychology rests on the "non-perceptible" (1970b, p. 268), in the modern nature "disappears" and is "opened up in depth" (p. 268)—"... life has left the tabulated space of order and become wild once more" (p. 278)—and needed to be tamed. Terman argued in 1920 that the methods of testing "transformed the 'science of trivialities' into the science of human engineering" (Samuelson, 1979, p. 107). The mind became "a surface for inscription of power" (Dreyfus & Rabinow, 1983, p. 149

Chapter 3

1. The next director of the LSE (Sir) Alexander Carr-Saunders, was also a social biologist with whom Hogben felt he was unlikely to get on. Carr-Saunders was on the Council of the Eugenics Education Society

from 1920, Editor of the Eugenics Review (1920–27), Vice-President of the Eugenics Society (1936–39) and its President (1949–53).
2. Allan (2005) writes tellingly about the "performance of care".
3. Perhaps here Foucault succumbs to the attractions of a linear, humanist history or illustrates "the ways in which we are entrapped and limited by prevalent uses of language and familiar grammatical constructions and sequencing of ideas and descriptions of 'strings of events'" (Felicity Armstrong, personal communication).
4. See www.idea.gov.uk/idk/core/page.do?pageId=7942796

Chapter 4

1. Foucault is not always consistent in his use of these terms.
2. This is the framework for the 1982–83 Lectures series *The Government of the Self and Others*.
3. As I signalled in Chapter 2 there is a whole set of genealogical work to be done on the idea of costs—in the economic sense (see Nealon, 2008, p. 17), in relation to the "costs" of oppression and in terms of the costs of speaking the truth and staying silent.

REFERENCES

Ahmed, S. (2004). Declarations of whiteness: the non-performativity of anti-racism. *borderlands e-journal*. Retrieved from: www.borderlands. net.au/vol3no2_2004/ahmed_declarations.htm

Ainscow, M., Booth, T. et al. (1999). Inclusion and exclusion in schools: Listening to some hidden voices. In K.Ballard (Ed.), *Inclusive education: international voices on disability and injustice*. London: Falmer Press.

Allan, J. (1999). *Actively seeking inclusion: pupils with special needs in mainstream schools*. London: Falmer Press.

Allan, J. (2003). *Inclusion for all? Scottish education: beyond devolution*. Edinburgh: University of Edinburgh Press.

Allan, J. (2005). Inclusion as an ethical project. In S.Tremain (Ed.), *Foucault and disability*. Ann Arbor, MI: University of Michigan Press.

Allan, J. (2008). Inclusion for all? *Scottish Education: Third edition: beyond devolution*. Edinburgh: Edinburgh University Press.

Apple, M. (2006). *Educating the right way: markets, standards, God and inequality*. New York: Routledge.

Apple, M. (2012). *Can education change society*? New York: Routledge.

Apple, M., & Pedroni, T. (2005). Conservative alliance building and African American support for voucher plans. *Teachers College Record*, 107(9), 2068–2105.

Armstrong, D. (2003). *Experiences of special education: re-evaluating policy and practice through life stories*. London: Routledge.

Armstrong, F. (2009). The historical development of special education: humanitarian rationality or 'wild profusion of entangled events?' *History of Education*, 31(5): 437–456.

Baker, B. (1998). 'Childhood' in the emergence and spread of U.S. public schools. In T. S.Popkewitz & M.Brennan (Eds.), *Foucault's challenge: discourse, knowledge and power in education*. New York: Teachers College Press.

Ball, S. J. (1993). What is policy? Texts, trajectories and toolboxes. *Discourse, 13*(2), 10–17.

Ball, S. J. (2012). *Global Education Inc.: new policy networks and the neoliberal imaginary*. London: Routledge.

Ball, S. J., Hull, R. et al. (1984). The tyranny of the Devil's mill: time and task in the school. In S.Delamont (Ed.), *Readings on interaction in the classroom*. London: Methuen.

Ball, S. J., Maguire, M. M. et al. (2011). Assessment technologies in schools: "deliverology" and the "play of dominations". *Research Papers in Education*. Published 18th March 2011 on iFirst.

Barker, M. (1981). *The new racism: conservatives and the ideology of the tribe*. London: Junction Books.

Barton, L., & Armstrong, F. (2007). *Policy, experience and change: cross-cultural reflections on inclusive education*. Dordrecht: Springer.

Bauman, Z. (1991). *Modernity and ambivalence*. Oxford: Polity Press.

Bauman, Z. (1996). Morality in the age of contingency. In P.Heelas, S.Lash, & P.Morris (Eds.), *Detraditionalization: critical reflections on authority and identity*. Oxford: Basil Blackwell.

Bauman, Z. (2004). Liquid sociality. In N. Gane (Ed.), *The future of social theory*. London: Continuum.

Benjamin, S. (2006). From "idiot child" to "mental defective": schooling and the production of intellectual disability in the UK 1850–1944. *Educate: The Journal of Doctoral Research in Education, 1*(1), 23–44.

Bennett, T. (1995). *The birth of the museum, history, theory, politics*. London: Routledge.

Bernstein, B. (1990). *The structuring of pedagogic discourse*. London: Routledge.

Bernstein, B. (2001a). From pedagogies to knowledges. In A.Morais, I.Neves, B.Davies, & H.Daniels (Eds.), *Towards a sociology of pedagogy*. New York: Peter Lang.

Bernstein, B. (2001b). Video conference with Basil Bernstein. In A.Morais, I.Neves, B.Davies, & H.Daniels (Eds.), *Towards a sociology of pedagogy*. New York: Peter Lang.

Bernstein, R. (1994). Foucault: critique as a philosophical ethos. In M.Kelly (Ed.), *Critique and power: recasting the Foucault/Habermas debate*. Cambridge, MA: MIT Press.

Besley, T. (2005). Foucault, truth telling and technologies of the self in schools. *Journal of Educational Enquiry, 6*(1), 76–89.

Blacker, D. (1998). Intellectuals at work and in power: towards a Foucauldian research ethic. In T. S.Popkewitz, & M.Brennan (Eds.), *Foucault's challenge: discourse, knowledge and power in education.* New York: Teachers College Press.

Bourdieu, P. (1986). *Distinction: a social critique of the judgement of taste.* London: Routledge.

Bourdieu, P., & Champagne, P. (1999). Outcasts on the inside. In P.Bourdieu (Ed.) *The weight of the world.* Cambridge: Polity Press.

Broadhead, L.-A., and Howard, S. (1998). 'The art of punishing': the Research Assessment Exercise and the ritualisation of power in higher education. *Education Policy Analysis Archives, 6*(8). Retrieved from http://epaa.asu.edu/epaa/v6n8.html

Burchell, G. (1996). Liberal government and techniques of the self. In A.Barry, T.Osborne, & N.Rose (Eds.), *Foucault and political reason.* London: UCL Press.

Burt, C. (1937). *The backward child.* London: University of London Press.

Butin, D. (2001). If this is resistance I would hate to see domination: retrieving Foucault's notion of resistance within educational research. *Educational Studies, 32*(2), 157–176.

Butler, J. (1990). *Gender trouble.* London: Routledge.

Butler, J. (2004). *Undoing gender.* New York and London: Routledge.

Charles, E. (1936). *The menace of underpopulation: a biological study of the decline of population.* London: Watts & Co.

Chitty, C. (2009). *Race, eugenics and intelligence in education.* London: Continuum.

Chomsky, N., Foucault, F. et al. (2006). *The Chomsky–Foucault debate: on human nature.* New York: The New Press.

Coard, B. (1971). *How the West Indian child is made educationally sub-normal by the British school system.* London: New Beacon Books.

Colley, H., James, D. et al. (2003). Learning as becoming in vocational education and training: class gender and the role of vocational habitus. *Journal of Vocational Education and Training, 55*(4), 471–496.

Cornwell, J. (2004). *Hitler's scientists: science, war and the Devil's pact.* Harmondsworth: Penguin.

Craft, M. (Ed.). (1970). *Family. class and education.* London: Longman.

Davidson, A. I. (2003). *Introduction to abnormal: lectures at the College de France 1974–1975. M. Foucault.* London: Verso.

Davies, B., & Petersen, E. B. (2005). Neo-liberal discourse and the academy: the forestalling of (collective) resistance. *Learning and Teaching in the Social Sciences, 2*(2), 77–98.

Deacon, R. (2006). From confinement to attachment: Michel Foucault on the rise of the school. *The European Legacy, 11*(2), 121–138.

Dean, M. (1991). *The constitution of poverty: toward a genealogy of liberal governance.* London: Routledge.

Dean, M. (1994). *Critical and effective histories. Foucault's methods and historical sociology.* London and New York: Routledge.

Dean, M. (1999). *Governmentality: power and rule in modern society.* London: Sage.

Dean, M. (2007). *Governing societies: political perspectives on domestic and international rule.* Maidenhead: Open University Press.

Defert, D., & Ewald, F. (Eds.). (2001). *Dits et Écrits 1954–1988. Vol. II, 1976–1988 Michel Foucault.* Paris: Gallimard.

Deleuze, G. (1995). *Gilles Deleuze's interview on Foucault, 'life as a work of art' negotiations: 1972–1990* (M. Joughin, Trans.). New York: Columbia University Press.

Department for Education. (2010). *The importance of teaching. The Schools' White Paper 2010.* Cm 7980, Department for Education.

Department for Education. (2011). *Support and aspiration: a new approach to special educational needs and disability.* Retrieved from London: www.eduation.gov.uk/../SEND%20Paper.pdf

Devine-Eller, A. (2004). Applying Foucault to Education. Retrieved from http://issuu.com/gfbertini/docs/applying_foucault_to_education

DfES (2005). *Higher standards better schools for all.* London: DfES.

Dillon, M., & Lobo-Guerrero, L. (2008). Biopolitics of security in the 21st century. *Review of International Studies, 34*(2), 265–292.

Donald, J. (1992). *Sentimental education: schooling, popular culture and the regulation of liberty.* New York: Verso.

Dreyfus, H. L., & Rabinow, P. (1983). *Michel Foucault: beyond structuralism and hermeneutics.* Chicago, IL: University of Chicago Press.

du Gay, P. (2004). Against "enterprise" (but not against "enterprise", for that would make no sense). *Organization, 11*(1), 37–57.

Dyhouse, C. (1983). Girls growing up in late Victorian and Edwardian England. *History, 68*(223), 268–374.

Edwards, R. (2002). Mobilizing lifelong learning: governmentality in educational practices. *Journal of Education Policy, 17*(3), 353–365.

Eggleston, J. (1976). Research in the sociology of education. *Paedagogica Europaea, 11*(1), 123–132.

Encyclopedia of Philosophy. Michel Foucault. Retrieved from www.iep.utm.edu/.

Eribon, D. (1991). *Michel Foucault.* Cambridge, MA: Harvard University Press.

Evans, J., Rich, E. et al. (2008). Body pedagogies, P/policy, health and gender. *British Educational Research Journal, 34*(3), 367–403.

Falk, C. (1999). Sentencing learners to life: retrofitting the academy for the information age. *Theory, Technology and Culture, 22*(1–2), 19–27.

Ferguson, A. A. (2000). *Bad boys public schools in the making of black masculinity.* Ann Arbor, MI: University of Michigan Press.

Floud, J. (1970). Social class factors in educational achievement. In M.Craft (Ed.), Family, class and education: a reader. London: Longman.

Flynn, T. R. (2005). *Satre, Foucault and historical reason vol 2: a poststructuralist mapping of history.* Chicago, IL: University of Chicago Press.

Foucault, M. (1970a). The order of discourse. Inaugural lecture at the Collège de France 2nd December 1970. In R.Young (Ed.), *Untying the text, a post-structuralist reader* (pp. 49–78). Boston, MA: Routledge and Kegan Paul.

Foucault, M. (1970b). *The order of things.* New York: Pantheon.

Foucault, M. (1972). *The archeology of knowledge.* New York: Vintage.

Foucault, M. (1974). *The archaeology of knowledge.* London: Tavistock.

Foucault, M. (1975). *I, Pierre Riviere, having slaughtered my mother, my sister and my brother.* Harmondsworth: Penguin.

Foucault, M. (1976 [1988]). *The history of sexuality vol. 1: the will to knowledge.* Harmondsworth: Penguin.

Foucault, M. (1977a). *Discipline and punish.* New York: Pantheon Press.

Foucault, M. (1977b). *Language, counter-memory, practice: selected essays and interviews.* Ithaca, NY: Cornell University Press.

Foucault, M. (1979). *Discipline and punish.* Harmondsworth: Peregrine.

Foucault, M. (1980a). *Power/knowledge: selected interviews and other writings.* New York: Pantheon.

Foucault, M. (1980b). *Two lectures. Power/knowledge.* C. Gordon. London: Longman.

Foucault, M. (1981). *The history of sexuality: an introduction.* Harmondsworth: Penguin.

Foucault, M. (1982). The subject and power: afterword to H. Dreyfus and P. Rabinow. In H.Dreyfus & P.Rabinow. *Michel Foucault: beyond structuralism and hermeneutics.* Chicago, IL: University of Chicago Press.

Foucault, M. (1983a). Discourse and truth: the problematization of Parrhesia: 6 lectures given by Michel Foucault at the University of California at Berkeley, Oct–Nov. 1983. Berkeley University. Retrieved from http://foucault.info/documents/parrhesia/

Foucault, M. (1983b). Interview: structuralism and poststructuralism. *Tehs 55,* 195–211.

Foucault, M. (1983c). On the genealogy of ethics: an overview of work in progress. In H.Dreyfus & P.Rabinow (Eds.), *Michel Foucault: beyond structuralism and hermeneutics.* Chicago, IL: University of Chicago Press.

Foucault, M. (1983d). Why study power: the question of the subject. In H.Dreyfus & P.Rabinow (Eds.), *Michel Foucault: beyond structuralism and hermeneutics.* Chicago, IL: University of Chicago Press.

Foucault, M. (1984a). Neitzsche, genealogy, history. In P.Rabinow (Ed.), *The Foucault reader.* London: Peregrine.

Foucault, M. (1984b). What is Enlightenment? (Qu'est-ce que les Lumières?). In P.Rabinow (Ed.), *The Foucault Reader* (pp. 32–50). New York: Pantheon Books.

Foucault, M. (1984 [1997]). Interview with Paul Rabinow. In *Volume 1 "Ethics" of "Essential Works of Foucault".* New York: The New Press.

Foucault, M. (1988a). *Michel Foucault: politics, philosophy and culture – interviews and other writings 1977–1984.* New York: Routledge.

Foucault, M. (1988b). *Politics, philosophy, culture: interviews and other writings 1972–1977.* New York: Routledge.

Foucault, M. (1988c). Power, moral values and the intellectual: an interview with Micheal Bess, San Fransisco, 3rd November 1980. *History of the Present 1–2,* 11–13.

Foucault, M. (1988d). Truth, power, self: an interview with Michel Foucault. In L. H.Martin, H.Gutman, & P.Hutton. *Technologies of the self.* Amherst, MA: The University of Massachusetts Press.

Foucault, M. (1991a). Questions of method. In G.Burchell, C.Gordon, & P.Miller (Eds.), *The Foucault effect: studies in governmentality.* Hemel Hempstead: Harvester/Wheatsheaf.

Foucault, M. (1991b). *Remarks on Marx: conversations with Duccio Trombadori.* New York: Semiotext(e).

Foucault, M. (1992). *The history of sexuality vol. 2: the use of pleasure.* Harmondsworth: Penguin.

Foucault, M. (1993). About the beginning of the hermeneutics of the self: two lectures at Dartmouth. *Political Theory 21*(2), 198–227.

Foucault, M. (1996). *Foucault live: collected interviews, 1961–84.* S.Lotringer (Ed.). New York: Semiotext(e).

Foucault, M. (1997a). Polemics, politics and problematizations an interview conducted by Paul Rabinow in May 1984. (L. Davis, Trans.), *Essential works of Foucault: volume 1 ethics.* New York: The New Press.

Foucault, M. (1997b). The ethics of the concern for self as a practice of freedom. In P.Rabinow (Ed.), *Michel Foucault: ethics, subjectivity and truth: the essential works of Michel Foucault 1954–1984, vol 1.* Harmondsworth: Penguin.

Foucault, M. (1997c). What is critique? (L. Hochrot, Trans.). In S.Lotringer & L.Hochroth (Eds.), *The politics of truth.* New York: Semiotext(e).

Foucault, M. (1997d). Writing the self. In A. Davidson (Ed.), *Foucault and his interlocutors.* Chicago: University of Chicago Press.

Foucault, M. (1998). What is an author. In P.Rabinow (Ed.), *Aesthetics, method, and epistemology.* New York: The Free Press.

Foucault, M. (2001a). *Fearless speech.* Los Angeles: Semiotext(e).

Foucault, M. (2001b). *Madness and civilization.* London: Routledge.

Foucault, M. (2003). *Abnormal: lectures at the College de France 1974–1975.* London: Verso.

Foucault, M. (2004a). *Society must be defended.* London: Penguin Books.

Foucault, M. (2004b). *The hermeneutics of the subject: lectures at the College de France 1981–82.* Basingstoke: Palgrave.

Foucault, M. (2006a). *Crise de la medicine ou crise de 'antimedicine'. Dits et écrits vol III*, pp. 40–58. Paris: Gallimard.

Foucault, M. (2006b). *Psychiatric power: lectures at the Collège de France, 1973–1974.* Basingstoke: Palgrave Macmillan.

Foucault, M. (2009). *Security, territory, population: lectures at the College de France 1977–78.* New York, Palgrave Macmillan.

Foucault, M. (2010a). *The birth of biopolitics: lectures at the College de France 1978–1979.* Basingstoke: Palgrave Macmillan.

Foucault, M. (2010b). *The government of the self and others: lectures at the College de France 1982–1983.* Basingstoke: Palgrave.

Foucault, M. (2012). *The history of sexuality, volume 3: the care of the self.* New York: Knopf Doubleday Publishing Group.

Foucault, M. (n.d.). Self-writing. Retrieved from itsy.co.uk/archive/sisn/Pos/green/Foucault.doc

Gale, T. (2001). Critical policy sociology: historiography, archaeology and genealogy as methods of policy analysis. *Journal of Education Policy, 16*(5), 379–393.

Gee, J. (1999). New people in new worlds: networks, the new capitalism and schools. In B.Cope & M.Kalantzis (Eds.), *Multiliteracies: literacy learning and the design of social futures.* London, Routledge.

Gillborn, D. (2010a). 'Reform, racism and the centrality of whiteness: assessment, ability and the 'new eugenics'. *Irish Educational Studies, 29*(3), 231–252.

Gillborn, D. (2010b). The white working class, racism and respectability: victims, degenerates and interest-convergence. *British Journal of Educational Studies, 58*(1), 3–25.

Gillborn, D., & Youdell, D. (2000). *Rationing education: policy, practice, reform and equity.* Buckingham: Open University Press.

Gillies, D. (2011). Agile bodies: a new imperative in neoliberal governance. *Journal of Education Policy, 26*(2), 207–223.

Gordon, C. (1991). Governmental Rationality: an introduction. In G. Burchell, C. Gordon & P. Miller (Eds.), *The Foucault Effect: studies in governmentality.* Brighton: Harvester/Wheatsheaf.

Gordon, C., Miller, P. et al., (Eds.). (1991). *The Foucault effect: studies in governmentality.* Brighton: Harvester/Wheatsheaf.

Graham, J. (2011). *An exploration of African-Caribbean boys' underachievement and their stories of schooling: their own worst enemies?* (Unpublished PhD thesis). School of Sport and Education. Brunel University, London.

Graham, L. J., and Slee, R. (2008). An illusory interiority: interrogating the discourse/s of inclusion. *Educational Philosophy and Theory, 40*(2), 247–260.

Green, B. (1998). Born-again teaching? Governmentality, "grammar" and public schooling. In T. S.Popkewitz & M.Brennan (Eds.), *Foucault's challenge: discourse, knowledge and power in education.* New York: Teachers College Press.

Gutting, G. (Ed.). (1994). *The Cambridge companion to Foucault.* Cambridge: Cambridge University Press.

Hacking, I. (1995). *Rewriting the soul: multiple personality and the sciences of memory.* Princeton, NJ: Princeton University Press.

Hall, S. (1989). Ethnicity, identity and difference. *Radical America, 23*(4), 9–20.

Harvey, D. (2005). *A brief history of neo-liberalism.* Oxford: Oxford University Press.

Hatcher, C. (1998). *Making the enterprising manager in Australia: a genealogy.* (Unpublished PhD thesis). School of Cultural and Policy Studies, Faculty of Education. Queensland University of Technology, Brisbane.

Haydon, G. (2004). Values education: sustaining the ethical environment. *Journal of Moral Education, 33*(2), 116–129.

Hernstein, R. J., & Murray, C. (1994). *The bell curve: intelligence and class structure in American life.* New York: The Free Press.

Higher Education Funding Council For England (HEFCE). (2009). *The research excellence framework: a brief guide to proposals (October).* London: HEFCE www.hefce.ac.uk/research/ref (accessed 2 June 2010).

Hill, V. (2005). Through the past darkly: a review of British Ability Scales. *Child and Adolescent Mental Health, 10*(2), 87–98.

Hogben, L. T. (Ed.). (1938). *Political arithmetic: a symposium of population studies.* London: G. Allen & Unwin Ltd.

Hoskin, K. (1990). Foucault under examination: the crypto-educationalist unmasked. In S. J.Ball (Ed.), *Foucault and education: disciplines and knowledge.* London: Routledge.

Humphries, S., & Gordon, P. (1992). *The experience of disability 1900–1950.* Plymouth: Northcote House.

Hunter, I. (1994). *Rethinking the school.* St Leonards: Allen and Unwin.

Hunter, I. (1996). Assembling the School. In A. Barry, T. Osborne & N. Rose (Eds.), *Foucault and political reason: Liberalism, neo-liberalism and rationalities of government.* London: UCL Press.

Hurt, J. S. (1988). *Outside the mainstream: A history of special education.* London: Batsford.

Hylton, K. (2009). *'Race' and sport: critical race theory.* London: Routledge.

Jessop, B. (2002). *The future of the capitalist state.* Cambridge: Polity.

Jones, D. (1990). The genealogy of the urban school teacher. In S. J. Ball (Ed.), *Foucault and education: Disciplines and knowledge.* London: Routledge.

Jones, D., & Ball, S. J. (1995). Michel Foucault and the discourse of education. In P. L.McLaren & J.Giarelli (Eds.), *Critical theory and educational research.* New York: SUNY Press.

Kay-Shuttleworth, J. (1862). *Four periods of public education as reviewed in 1832 – 1839 – 1846–1862 in papers.* London: Longman, Green, Longman, and Roberts.

Keep, E. (1997). 'There's no such thing as society...': some problems with an individual approach to creating a learning society. *Journal of Education Policy, 12*(6), 457–471.

Kelly, P. (2006). The entrepreneurial self and 'youth-at-risk': exploring the horizons of identity in the 21st century. *Journal of Youth Studies, 9*(1), 17–32.

Keynes, J. M. (1946). Opening remarks: the Galton lecture. *Eugenics Review, 38*(1), 39–40.

King, D., and R. Hansen. (1999). Experts at work: state autonomu, social learning and eugenic sterilization in 1930s Britain. *British Journal of Political Science, 29*(1), 77–107.

Ladson-Billings, G. (2009). Just what is critical race theory? In E.Taylor, D.Gillborn, & G.Ladson-Billings (Eds.), *Foundations of critical race theory.* New York and London: Routledge.

Larsen, M. A. (2011). *The making and shaping of the victorial teacher: a comparative new cultural history*. Basingstoke: Palgrave Macmillan.

Lazzarato, M. (2009). Neoliberalism in action: inequality, insecurity and the reconstitution of the social. *Theory, Culture and Society, 26*(6), 109–133.

Lee, A., & J. Hills (1998). *New Cycles of Disadvantage?* Report of a conference organised by CASE on behalf of ESRC for HM Treasury. Swindon: ESRC.

Lemke, T. (2000). Foucault, governmentality, and critique. Paper presented at the Rethinking Marxism Conference, University of Amherst (MA). Retrieved from http://www.andosciasociology.net/resources/Foucault$2C+Governmentality$2C+and+Critique+IV-2.pdf

Leys, M. (2001). *Market-driven politics*. London: Verso.

Lowe, R. (1998). The educational impact of the eugenics movement – eugenics and the declining birth rate in twentieth century Britain. *International Journal of Educational Research, 27*(8), 647–660.

Lyotard, J.-F. (1984). *The postmodern condition: a report on knowledge*. Manchester: Manchester University Press.

MacNaughton, G. (2005). *Doing Foucault in early childhood studies: applying poststructural ideas*. London: Routledge.

Mahon, M. (1992). *Foucault's Nietzscean genealogy: truth, power and the subject*. Albany, NY: SUNY.

Marshall, J. (1989). Foucault and education. *Australian Journal of Education, 2*(1), 97–111.

Martin, L. H., Gutman, H. et al., (Eds.). (1988). *Technologies of the self: a seminar with Michel Foucault*. London: Tavistock.

Maudsley, H. (1867). *The psychology and pathology of mind*. London: MacMillan.

McCulloch, G. (2011). Sensing the realities of english middle-class education: James Bryce and the schools inquiry commission 1865–1868. *History of Education, 40*(5), 599–613.

McGushin, E. (2011). Foucault's theory and practice of subjectivity. In D. Taylor (Ed.), *Michel Foucault: Key concepts*. Durham: Acumen.

McNay, L. (1994). *Foucault: A critical introduction*. Polity Press: Cambridge.

Mendieta, E. (2011). The practice of freedom. In D.Taylor (Ed.), *Michel Foucault: key concepts*. Durham: Acumen.

Midelfort, H. C. E. (1980). Madness and civilization in early modern Europe: a reappraisal of Michel Foucault. In B. C.Malament (Ed.), *After the reformation: essays in honor of J.H. Hexter*. Baltimore, MD: University of Pennsylvania Press.

Miller, P., & N. Rose (2008). *Governing the Present*. Cambridge: Polity Press.

Mills, S. (2003). *Michel Foucault*. London: Routledge.

Mirza, H. S. (1998). Race, gender and IQ: the social consequence of a pseudo-scientific discourse. *Race Ethnicity and Education, 1*(1), 109–126.

Musgrove, F. (1970). The good home. In M.Craft (Ed.), *Family, class and education: a reader*. London: Longman.

Nealon, J. T. (2008). *Foucault beyond Foucault*. Stanford, CA: Stanford University Press.

Norwood Report, T. (1943). *Curriculum and examinations in secondary schools*. London: HM Stationery Office.

O'Flynn, G., and Petersen, E. B. (2007). The 'good life' and the 'rich portfolio': young women, schooling and neo-liberal subjectification. *British Journal of Sociology of Education, 28*(4), 459–472.

Oksala, J. (2007). *How to read Foucault*. London: Granta Books.

Olssen, M. (1993). Science and individualism in educational psychology: problems for practice and points of departure. *Educational Psychology, 13*(2), 155–172.

Olssen, M. (2006). *Michel Foucault: materialism and education*. London: Paradigm.

Olssen, M. (2011). The strange death of the liberal university: research assessments and the impact of research. In R.King, S.Marginson, & R. Naidoo (Eds.), *A handbook of globalisation and higher education*. Cheltenham: Edward Elgar.

O'Malley, P. (1996). Risk and responsibility. In A. Barry, T. Osborne, & N. Rose (Eds.), *Foucault and political reason: Liberalism, neo-liberalism and rationalities of government*. London: UCL Press.

Ozga, J. (1998). The entrepreneurial researcher: re-formations of identity in the research marketplace. *International Studies in Sociology of Education, 8*(2), 143–153.

Ozga, J. (2008). Governing knowledge: research steering and research quality. *European Educational Research Journal, 7*(3), 261–272.

Ozga, J. (2009). Governing education through data in England: from regulation to self-evaluation. *Journal of Education Policy, 24*(2), 149–163.

Peck, J. (2003). Geography and public policy: mapping the penal state. *Progress in Human Geography, 27*(2), 222–232.

Perryman, J. (2007). Inspection and emotion. *Cambridge Journal of Education, 37*(2), 173–190.

Perryman, J., Ball, S. J. et al. (2011). Life in the pressure cooker – School league tables and English and mathematics teachers. *British Journal of Educational Studies, 59*(2), 179–195.

Peters, M. (2000). Writing the self: Wittgenstein, confession and pedagogy. *Journal of Philosophy of Education, 34*(2), 353–368.

Peters, M. (2001). Education, Enterprise Culture and the Entrepreneurial Self: A Foucualdian Perspective. *Journal of Educational Enquiry,* 2(2), 58–71.

Peters, M. (2003). Truth-telling as an Educational Practice of the Self: Foucault, Parrhesia and the ethics of subjectivity. *Oxford Review of Education,* 29(2), 207–224.

Peters, M. A., & Besley, T. (Eds.). (2007). *Why Foucault? New directions in educational research.* New York: Peter Lang.

Pignatelli, F. (1993). What can I do? Foucault on freedom and the question of teacher agency. *Educational Theory,* 43(4), 411–432.

Popkewitz, T. S., & Brennan, M. (Eds.). (1998). *Foucault's challenge: discourse, knowledge and power in education.* New York: Teachers College Press.

Prado, C. G. (1995). *Starting with Foucault: an introduction to genealogy.* Boulder, CO: Westview Press.

Pritchard, D. G. (1963). *Education and the handicapped 1760–1960.* London: Routledge and Kegan Paul.

Rabinow, P., and Rose, N. (2003). Foucault today. In P.Rabinow & N.Rose (Eds.), *The essential works of Michel Foucault.* New York: New Press.

Rausch, C. (2012). *Fixing children: producing a hierarchy of learners in primary school processes.* History and Social Science Department, Institute of Education, University of London. PhD thesis.

Revel, J. (2008). *Dictionnaire Foucault.* Paris: ellipses.

Ringrose, J. (2011). *Post-feminist education? Girls and the sexual politics of schooling.* London: Routledge.

Rinne, R., Kallo, J. et al. (2004). Too eager to comply? OECD education policies and the Finnish response. *European Educational Research Journal,* 2(2), 454–485.

Roberts, R. (1973). *The Classic Slum: Salford Life in the First Quarter of the Century.* Harmondsworth: Pelican.

Rorty, R. (1982). *The consequences of pragmatism.* Minneapolis, MN: University of Minnesota Press.

Rose, N. (1996). Governing "advanced" liberal democracies. In A.Barry, T.Osborne, & N.Rose (Eds.), *Foucault and political reason: liberalism, neo-liberalism and rationalities of government.* London: UCL Press.

Rose, N. (1998). *Inventing ourselves.* Cambridge: Polity Press.

Rose, N. (1999). *Powers of freedom: reframing political thought.* Cambridge: Cambridge University Press.

Rose, N., & Novas, C. (2004). Biological citizenship. In A.Ong & S.Collier (Eds.), *Global assemblages: technology, politics and ethics as anthropological problems* (pp. 439–463). Oxford: Blackwell.

Roth, M. S. (1981). Foucault's "history of the present". *History and Theory*, 20(1), 32–46.

Samuelson, F. (1979). Putting Psychology on the Map: Ideology and Intelligence Testing. In A. R. Buss (Ed.), *Psychology in a Social Context*. New York: Irvington.

Sawicki, J. (1991). *Disciplining Foucault: feminism, power and the body*. New York, Routledge.

Scheurich, J. J. (1994). Policy archaeology: a new policy studies methodology. *Journal of Education Policy*, 9(4), 297–316.

Scull, A. T. (1979). *Museums of madness: the social organization of insanity in 19th century England*. Harmondsworth: Penguin Books.

Selden, S. (1999). *Inheriting the shame: the story of eugenics and racism in America*. New York: Teachers College Press.

Sewell, D. (2009). How eugenics poisoned the welfare state. *The Spectator*, 25 November.

Shapiro, M. (1992). *Reading the post-modern polity*. Minneapolis, MN: University of Minnesota Press.

Shein, A. (2004). A Foucauldian explanation of racism beyond Foucault's. Retrieved from http://www.panopticweb.com/2004conference/3.shein.pdf

Sheridan, A. (1980). *Michel Foucault: the will to truth*. London: Tavistock.

Shoen, J. (2005). *Women and the politics of sterilization: an introduction to the history of North Carolina's eugenics program*. Durham, NC: University of North Carolina Press.

Shore, C., & Wright, S. (1999). Audit culture and anthropology: neo-liberalism in British higher education. *The Journal of the Royal Anthropological Institute*, 5(4), 557–575.

Simons, J. (1995). *Foucault and the political*. London: Routledge.

Simons, M., & Masschelien, J. (2006). The permanent quality tribunal in education and the limits of education policy. *Policy Futures in Education*, 4(3), 294–307.

Sims, G. R. (1883). *How the Poor Live*. London: Chatto.

Slater, D., & Tonkiss, F. (2001). *Market society*. Cambridge: Polity Press.

Slee, R. (1997). Imported or important theory? Sociological interrogations of disablement and special education. *British Journal of Sociology in Education*, 18(3), 407–419.

Slee, R. (2011). *The irregular school: exclusion, schooling, and inclusive education*. London: Routledge.

Slee, R., & Allan, J. (Eds.). (2008). *Doing inclusive educational research*. London: Sense.

Smith, R. (2007). *Being human: historical knowledge and the creation of human nature.* New York: Columbia University Press.

Spektorowski, A., & Mizrachi, E. (2004). Eugenics and the welfare state in Sweden: the politics of margins and the ideas of a productive society. *Journal of Contemporary History, 39*(3), 333–352.

Stobart, G. (2008). *Testing times: the uses and abuses of assessment.* London: Routledge.

Stoler, A. L. (1995). *Race and the education of desire: Foucault's history of sexuality and the colonial order of things.* Durham, NC: Duke University Press.

Tamboukou, M. (2003). *Women, education and the self: a Foucauldian perspective.* Basingstoke: Palgrave Macmillan.

Tamboukou, M. (2012). Truth telling Foucault and Arendt: Parrhesia, the pariah and academics in dark times. *Journal of Education Policy.* Published in iFirst on 10th July 2012.

Tamboukou, M., & Ball, S. J. (Eds.). (2004). *Dangerous encounters: genealogy and ethnography. eruptions.* New York: Peter Lang.

Tate, T. (1857). *The Philosophy of Education; or, the Principles and Parctice of Teaching.* London: Longman, Brown, Green, Longmans and Roberts.

Taylor, C. (1986). Foucault on freedom and truth. In C.Hoy (Ed.), *Foucault: a critical reader.* Oxford: Blackwell.

Taylor, D. (2011). Practices of the self. In D. Taylor. (Ed.) *Michel Foucault: Key Concepts.* Durham: Acumen.

Terman, L. M. (1916). *The uses of intelligence tests.* Boston, MA: Houghton Mifflin.

Thaler, R. H., & Sunstein, C. R. (2008). *Nudge: improving decisions about health, wealth, and happiness.* New Haven, CT: Yale University Press.

The Radnor Report (1908). Feeble-Minded (1904–1908) Cd. 4202. London: HMSO.

Thorndike, E. L. (1922). *The psychology of arithmetic.* New York: Macmillan.

Tilton, J. (2000). *Dangerous or endangered?: race and the politics of youth in urban America.* New York: New York University Press.

Troyna, B. (1994). The 'everyday world' of teachers? Deracialised discourses in the sociology of teachers and the teaching profession. *British Journal of Sociology of Education, 15*(3), 325–339.

Tyler, I. (2006). Chav mum, chav scum: class disgust in contemporary Britain. *Feminist Media Studies, 8*(1), 17–34.

Vander Schee, C. (2009). Fruit, vegetables, fatness, and Foucault: governing students and their families through school health policy. *Journal of Education Policy, 24*(5), 557–574.

Venn, C., & Terranova, T. (2009). Introduction: thinking after Michel Foucault. *Theory, Culture and Society, 26*(6), 1–11.

Veyne, P. (2010). *Foucault: his thought, his character.* Cambridge: Polity Press.

Vincent, C. (2012). *Parenting: responsibilities, risk and respect.* London: IOE Press.

Walzer, M. (1984). *Spheres of justice: a defence of pluralism and equality.* Oxford: Martin Robertson.

Warnock, M. (1978). *Special educational needs: committee of enquiry into the education of handicapped children.* London: HMSO.

Welshman, J. (n.d.). *The cycle of deprivation: myths and misconceptions.* Lancaster: University of Lancaster. Retrieved from http://www.longviewuk.com/pages/documents/PQcycle.pdf

White, H. (1978). *Tropics of discourse: essays in cultural criticism.* Baltimore, MD: Johns Hopkins University Press

White, J. (2006). *Intelligence, destiny and education: the ideological roots of intelligence testing.* London: Routledge.

Wilson, D. (2007). *America's new black ghetto.* New York: Taylor & Francis.

Wittel, A. (2001). Towards a network sociality. *Theory, Culture and Society, 18*(6), 51–76.

Youdell, D. (2006). *Impossible bodies, impossible selves: exclusions and student subjectivities.* Dordrecht: Springer.

Youdell, D. (2011). *School trouble: identity, power and politics in education.* London: Routledge.

INDEX

Introductory Note

References such as "138–9" indicate (not necessarily continuous) discussion of a topic across a range of pages. Wherever possible in the case of topics with many references (but not in the case of cited authors), these have either been divided into sub-topics or only the most significant discussions of the topic are listed. Because the entire volume is about the "Foucault", "power" and "education", the use of these terms (and certain others occurring throughout the work) as entry points has been restricted. Information will be found under the corresponding detailed topics.